A VERY PRESENT HELP

LIFE MESSAGES OF
GREAT CHRISTIANS

A Very Present Help

AMY CARMICHAEL

Compiled by
JUDITH COUCHMAN

Servant Publications
Ann Arbor, Michigan

Vine Books is an imprint of Servant Publications especially designed to serve evangelical Christians.

All Scripture quotations, unless indicated, are taken from the macBible ®1987, 1988, 1991, 1993 by The Zondervan Corporation. Macintosh is a trademark of Apple Computer, Inc. New Revised Standard Version of the Bible (NRSV) was copyrighted 1989 by the Division of Christian Education of the National Council of Churches of Christ in the United States of America, and used by permission. All rights reserved. The New International Version of the Bible (NIV) was copyrighted 1973, 1978, 1984 by The International Bible Society. All rights reserved.

The publisher wishes to thank the Christian Literature Crusade and Dohnavur Fellowship, UK, for permission to reprint excerpts of Amy Carmichael's writings. Copyright on these works is held by the Christian Literature Crusade, Fort Washington, PA 19034. Used by permission. All rights reserved.

Published by Servant Publications
P.O. Box 8617
Ann Arbor, Michigan 48107

Cover design: Hile Illustration and Design, Ann Arbor, Michigan

96 97 98 99 00   10 9 8 7 6 5 4 3 2 1

Printed in the United States of America
ISBN 0-89283-978-3

LIBRARY OF CONGRESS CATALOGING-IN-PUBLICATION DATA

Carmichael, Amy, 1867-1951.
A very present help / Amy Carmichael : compiled by Judith Couchman.
    p.   cm.
    ISBN 0-89283-978-3 — (Life messages of great Christians series ; 1)
    1. Spiritual life—Christianity—Meditations.   2. Devotional calendars.
I. Couchman, Judith.   II. Title.
BV4832.2.C272   1996   96-26543
242—dc20   CIP

For Shirley,
a sister and prayer warrior
whom I love and cherish.

Contents

Acknowledgments

~

YEARS AGO WHEN I FIRST READ Amy Carmichael's writings, I never dreamed that one day I'd be editing a portion of her works. It's a privilege, and for this honor I thank Bert Ghezzi at Servant Publications for believing in me and the *Life Messages of Great Christians* series.

I also thank Christian Literature Crusade for its help and generosity in granting the rights to reprint from Amy's works and Liz Heaney and Traci Mullins for their editing expertise.

As always, I thank these praying women for supporting me through another book: Charette Barta, Opal Couchman, Win Couchman, Madalene Harris, Karen Hilt, Shirley Honeywell, Mae Lammers, and Nancy Lemons.

Introduction

As a young teenager I walked the mile to and from junior high, hoping that on the way home I could stop at my friend Inez's house. Though twenty years older than me, I felt drawn to this woman because we shared common interests: our Christian faith, artistic endeavors, and particularly a love of books and writing. She listened to my dreams about becoming a writer and actually believed in them.

So when Inez handed me a slim volume to read, I paid attention. The navy-with-gold-lettered cover fit in my palm, but size proved the only "small" aspect of this book. The brief messages inside enlarged my soul with truths about God and a personal, conversational relationship with Him, written by a British-born missionary involved in a deep and meaningful relationship with the Creator.

The author was Amy Carmichael, and her book, *His Thoughts Said... His Father Said...*, affected me deeply. I wanted to know God as she did. Now that I'm an author, I'd also love for my work to flourish as long as Amy's has. For about sixty years her writings have inspired and challenged Christians to grow deeper in God and trust Him completely during life's difficulties.

Amy Carmichael arrived in India in 1895 and ministered there until her death in 1951. She constructed the groundwork for the Dohnavur Fellowship, a community dedicated to rescuing young girls from temple prostitution. After years of faithful service, Amy—called "Amma" by those who knew and loved her—suffered an accident, followed by an illness, that confined her to a bedroom for the rest of her life.

During those twenty pain-filled years, Amy imparted spiritual lessons to the Dohnavur family through written or dictated notes. Thankfully for us, many of those lessons, along with her poems, were published in books still in print today.

Because she faced much suffering as both an active missionary and a bedridden invalid, Amy often wrote of God as our "very present help" (Psalms 46:1) while passing through difficulty. And though occasionally her style and language feel outdated, the message remains refreshingly relevant. Repeatedly Amy reminds us that our unchangeable God is constant in His love, help, and compassion toward us, especially during times of pain and trial.

I pray this ever-green message will envelop and encourage you as, day by day, Amy's insights enter your life. May you find them—and our powerful God—a very present help indeed.

—*Judith Couchman*
November 1995

PART ONE

IN ACCEPTANCE LIES PEACE

He said, "I will forget the dying faces;
The empty places,
They shall be filled again.
O voices moaning deep within me, cease."
But in vain the word; vain, vain:
Not in forgetting lieth peace.

He said, "I will crowd action upon action,
The strife of faction
Shall stir me and sustain;
O tears that down the fire of manhood, cease."
But vain the word; vain, vain:
Not in endeavor lieth peace.

He said, "I will withdraw me and be quiet,
why meddle in life's riot?
Shut be my door to pain.
Desire, thou doest befool me, thou shalt cease."
But vain the word; vain, vain:
Not in aloofness lieth peace.

He said, "I will submit; I am defeated.
God hath depleted
My life of its rich gain.
O futile murmurings, why will ye not cease?"
But vain the word; vain, vain:
Not in submission lieth peace.

He said, "I will accept the breaking sorrow
Which God tomorrow
Will to His son explain."
Then did the turmoil deep within him cease.
Not vain the word, not vain;
For in Acceptance lieth peace.

"IN ACCEPTANCE LIETH PEACE," *TOWARD JERUSALEM*

AMY CARMICHAEL'S INSIGHT

When you accept rather than fight your circumstances
—even though you don't understand them—
you open your heart's gate to God's
love, peace, joy and contentment.

THE GOD OF SUN AND SNOW

THOUGHT FOR TODAY

God will not fail you during the Winter seasons of your life.

WISDOM FROM SCRIPTURE

I remember my affliction and my wandering, the bitterness and the gall. I well remember them, and my soul is downcast within me.

Yet this I call to mind and therefore I have hope: Because of the LORD's great love we are not consumed, for his compassions never fail. They are new every morning; great is your faithfulness.

I say to myself, "The LORD is my portion; therefore I will wait for him."

The LORD is good to those whose hope is in him, to the one who seeks him; it is good to wait quietly for the salvation of the LORD.

It is good for a man to bear the yoke while he is young. Let him sit alone in silence, for the LORD has laid it on him. Let him bury his face in the dust—there may yet be hope.

Let him offer his cheek to one who would strike him, and let him be filled with disgrace. For men are not cast off by the LORD forever. Though he brings grief, he will show compassion, so great is his unfailing love. For he does not willingly bring affliction or grief to the children of men.

LAMENTATIONS 3:19-33, NIV

Insights from Amy Carmichael

Note: Amy wrote this introductory essay to accompany a creative photo of a bush in wintertime.

You were a leafy bush, and many little things came to you for shelter. You were not great or important, but you could help those little things. And it was the joy of your life to help them.

Now you cannot do anything at all. Some desolation, illness, poverty, or something that you cannot talk about, has overwhelmed you, and all your green leaves have gone. So you cannot shelter even the least little bird; you are like this bush with its bare twigs, no use to anyone—that is what you think.

But look again at this bare bush. Look at the delicate tracery of lines on the snow. The sun is shining behind the bush, and so every little twig is helping to make something that is very beautiful. Perhaps other eyes, that you do not see, are looking on it too, wondering at what can be made of sun and snow and poor bare twigs. And the Spring will come again, for after Winter there is always Spring.

When will the Spring come? When will your bush be green with leaves again? When will the little birds you love come back to you? I do not know. I only know that sun and snow are working together for good; and the day will come when the very memory of helplessness to help, and barrenness, and poverty and loneliness will pass as a dream of the night; and all that seemed lost will be restored.

Now, in the multitude of the sorrows that you have in your heart, let these comforts refresh your soul. They will not fail you for He will not fail you who is the God of the sun and the snow.

—Figures of the True

QUESTIONS TO CONSIDER

1. What difficulty has ushered a Winter season into your life?

2. Based on today's Scripture, how can you cultivate the faith that Spring will come again?

A PRAYERFUL RESPONSE

Lord, even though this Winter season is difficult, please help me to "wait quietly for Your salvation." Amen.

IN HIS CARE

THOUGHT FOR TODAY

During times of trial, God wants to express His loving-kindness to you.

WISDOM FROM SCRIPTURE

To you, O LORD, I lift up my soul; in you I trust, O my God. Do not let me be put to shame, nor let my enemies triumph over me.

No one whose hope is in you will ever be put to shame, but they will be put to shame who are treacherous without excuse.

Show me your ways, O LORD, teach me your paths; guide me in your truth and teach me, for you are God my Savior, and my hope is in you all day long.

Remember, O LORD, your great mercy and love, for they are from of old. Remember not the sins of my youth and my rebellious ways; according to your love remember me, for you are good, O LORD.

Good and upright is the LORD; therefore he instructs sinners in his ways. He guides the humble in what is right and teaches them his way.

All the ways of the LORD are loving and faithful for those who keep the demands of his covenant.

For the sake of your name, O LORD, forgive my iniquity, though it is great.

Who, then, is the man that fears the LORD? He will instruct him in the way chosen for him. He will spend his days in prosperity, and his descendants will inherit the land.

The LORD confides in those who fear him; he makes his covenant known to them.

My eyes are ever on the LORD, for only he will release my feet from the snare.   PSALMS 25:1-15, NIV

INSIGHTS FROM AMY CARMICHAEL

Trials are not "chastisement." No earthly father goes on chastising a loving child. That is a common thought about suffering, but I am quite sure it is a wrong thought. Paul's sufferings were not that, nor are yours. They are battle wounds. They are signs of high confidence—honors. The Father holds His children very close to His heart when they are going through such rough places as this.

"Thy *care* hath preserved my spirit" (Job 10:12)—a lovely Revised Version (RV) margin note which helped me a few days ago—is my word for you. Think of it: All day long you are being cared for, you are *in* His care.

"All the paths of the Lord are loving-kindness" (Psalms 25:10). I also found that in RV lately and have found it feeds. *All* does not mean "all but these paths we are in now" or "nearly all, but perhaps not just this specially difficult, painful one."

All means *all.*

So your path with its unexplained sorrow, and mine with its unexplained sharp flints and briers, and both with their unexplained perplexity of guidance, their sheer mystery, are just loving-kindness, nothing less.

I am resting my heart on that word. It bears one up on eagle's wings; it gives courage and song and sweetness too, the sweetness

19

of spirit which it is death to lose even for one half hour.

Am I not enough, Mine own?

Enough, Mine own, for thee?…

Am I not enough, Mine own?

I forever and alone,

I, needing *thee?*

It was a long time before I could honestly say "Yes" to that question. I remember the turmoil of soul as if it were yesterday, but at last, oh the rest, "for in acceptance lieth peace."

Don't be surprised if temptations come: The one way is to throw yourself, everything you have to give, into the service to which you have been called. Paul spoke of himself as an offering poured out on "the sacrifice and service of your faith" (Philippians 2:17). That's what you must be, nothing kept back.

And as you give all, you find all.

Often His call is to follow in paths we would not have chosen. But if in truth we say, "Anywhere, Lord," He takes us at our word and orders our goings, and then He puts a new song in our mouths, even a thanksgiving unto our God (Psalms 40:2-3, Prayer Book Version).

There is wonderful joy to be had from knowing that we are *not* in the way of our own choice. At least I have found it so. It gives a peculiar sort of confidence that even we—we who are nothings—are being "ordered" in our goings. It is very good to be "ordered" by our beloved Lord.   —*Candles in the Dark*

Questions to Consider

1. In what ways do Amy's insights change your perspective on your own spiritual journey?

2. How might God be expressing His care for you by "ordering your way" in a direction you didn't expect?

A Prayerful Response

Lord, help me to say, "Anywhere, Lord," and to recognize Your loving-kindness toward me. Amen.

DON'T BE SURPRISED

THOUGHT FOR TODAY

Don't be surprised if you're under spiritual attack: It is the mark of the cross.

WISDOM FROM SCRIPTURE

Your attitude should be the same as that of Christ Jesus: Who, being in very nature God, did not consider equality with God something to be grasped, but made himself nothing, taking the very nature of a servant, being made in human likeness. And being found in appearance as a man, he humbled himself and became obedient to death—even death on a cross!

Therefore God exalted him to the highest place and gave him the name that is above every name, that at the name of Jesus every knee should bow, in heaven and on earth and under the earth, and every tongue confess that Jesus Christ is Lord, to the glory of God the Father.

Therefore, my dear friends, as you have always obeyed—not only in my presence, but now much more in my absence—continue to work out your salvation with fear and trembling, for it is God who works in you to will and to act according to his good purpose.

Do everything without complaining or arguing, so that you may become blameless and pure, children of God without fault in a crooked and depraved generation, in which you shine like stars in the universe as you hold out the word of life—in order that I may boast on the day of Christ that I did not run or labor for nothing.

But even if I am being poured out like a drink offering on

the sacrifice and service coming from your faith, I am glad and rejoice with all of you.

So you too should be glad and rejoice with me.

PHILIPPIANS 2:5-18, NIV

INSIGHTS FROM AMY CARMICHAEL

Don't be surprised if there is an attack on your work, on *you* who are called to do it, on your innermost nature—the hidden person of the heart. It must be so. The great thing is not to be surprised, nor to count it strange—for that plays into the hand of the enemy.

Is it possible that anyone should set himself to exalt our beloved Lord and *not* instantly become a target for many arrows? The very fact that your work depends utterly on Him and can't be done for a moment without Him calls for a very close walk and a constant communion of spirit. This alone is enough to account for anything the enemy can do.

But there are limits set. Greater is He. I have just read the glorious word in Romans 5:17: "They that receive the abundance of grace... reign in life, through the One, even Jesus Christ." And this was written to slaves in Nero's wicked palace. What daring faith the Spirit gave to Paul.

It *costs* to have a pure work. Not for nothing is our God called a consuming fire.

Don't be surprised if you suffer. It is part of the way of the cross. Mark 9:12 says, "The Son of Man must suffer much." If we follow in the way He went, we also must suffer.

You will find this truer every year as you go on. And anything is easier. Scourging is easier. "He must suffer many things, and" (as if this had to be mentioned specifically) *"be set at naught."*

Have you ever gone through your New Testament, marking the places where suffering in one form or another is mentioned? It's wonderfully enlightening. The Book is full of joy, but it is also full of pain, and pain is taken for granted. "Think it not strange. Count it all joy" (1 Peter 4:12; James 1:2).

We are meant to follow in His steps, not avoid them. What if our suffering is caused by those whom we love? Was *His* not caused by those whom He loved? Oh, what a Book the Bible is! If only we steep our souls in its mighty comfort we can't go far wrong; we shall never lose heart. "For hereunto were ye called: because Christ also suffered for you, leaving you an example, that ye should follow his steps" (1 Peter 2:21).

You will find that the joy of the Lord comes as you go on in the way of the cross. It was One who had nobody all his own on earth who said, "If I am offered upon the sacrifice and service of your faith, I joy, and rejoice" (Philippians 2:17). It is no small gift of His love, this opportunity to be offered upon the sacrifice and service—something you would not naturally choose, something that asks for more than you would naturally give.

So rejoice! You are giving Him what He asks you to give Him: the chance to show you what He can do.   —*Candles in the Dark*

Questions to Consider

1. In what specific ways are you or your work for God being attacked by evil spiritual forces?

2. How can Amy's insights help you rejoice in your suffering?

A Prayerful Response

Lord, please grant me Your joy and peace as I am poured out in Your service. Amen.

DAY 4

BEGINNING TO SINK

THOUGHT FOR TODAY

When you begin to sink, God immediately holds out His rescuing hand.

WISDOM FROM SCRIPTURE

Immediately Jesus made the disciples get into the boat and go on ahead of him to the other side, while he dismissed the crowd.

After he had dismissed them, he went up on a mountainside by himself to pray. When evening came, he was there alone, but the boat was already a considerable distance from land, buffeted by the waves because the wind was against it.

During the fourth watch of the night Jesus went out to them, walking on the lake. When the disciples saw him walking on the lake, they were terrified. "It's a ghost," they said, and cried out in fear.

But Jesus immediately said to them: "Take courage! It is I. Don't be afraid."

"Lord, if it's you," Peter replied, "tell me to come to you on the water."

"Come," he said. Then Peter got down out of the boat, walked on the water and came toward Jesus. But when he saw the wind, he was afraid and, beginning to sink, cried out, "Lord, save me!"

Immediately Jesus reached out his hand and caught him. "You of little faith," he said, "why did you doubt?" And when they climbed into the boat, the wind died down.

Then those who were in the boat worshiped him, saying, "Truly you are the Son of God."   MATTHEW 14:22-33, NIV

INSIGHTS FROM AMY CARMICHAEL

Beginning to sink… immediately. There are times when nothing comes to mind but these words. They assure us of so much more than they seem to say that their riches of comfort cannot be condensed into a page.

Chiefly they bring the certainty that there will be no sinking, for Peter never sank. "When I said, My foot slippeth," in that very moment "Thy mercy, O Lord, held me up" (Psalms 94:18). They come underneath the feeling of sinking; they say, "This shall never be!"

"And immediately Jesus stretched forth His hand and caught him" (Matthew 14:31). How many seconds lie between a man's beginning to sink and his sinking? A single second or less, I suppose. How swift, then, was the movement of love! And as He was, so He is.

"Must we wait till the evening to be forgiven?" a child once asked.

Do we not all know that feeling? It seems too good to be true that at the very moment of the sorrowful consciousness of sin, or even the shadow of sin, there is pardon, cleansing, the light of His blessed countenance. But nothing can ever be too good to be true with such a Lord as ours.

The use of the word "immediately" has been life and peace to me of late. It was Christ's sorely tried prisoner, Samuel Rutherford, who wrote that the parings and crumbs of glory, a shower like a thin May-mist of his Lord's love, was enough to make him green and sappy and joyful. Such a word, even such a little word as this, if only we open our hearts to its healing power, may be a crumb of glory, enlightening the soul, a thin May-mist of His love making green and sappy (or glowing and golden) what was so dry and dull before.

They were troubled, those poor men in the boat. "And immediately He talked with them" (verse 27). How needless their trouble seems to us as we read. Does ours seem as needless to the heavenly watchers? Do they wonder about us, as we do about those men, how there could be room for trouble in a ship that was under His command? (It was He who had constrained them to go to the other side. It is He who directs our boat now to the Other Side.) But there is nothing of this wonder in the sweetness of the words of our Lord Jesus when immediately He talked with them. He understood.

We who know how upholding loving words can be, when a friend does not blame, but just understands even the trouble that need not be, and comforts it. We can find honey in this honeycomb: "Immediately Jesus stretched forth His hand and caught Him."

"My soul hangeth upon Thee: Thy right hand upholdeth me" (Psalms 63:8).

"Immediately He talked with them" (Matthew 14:27).

"Speak, Lord: for Thy servant heareth" (1 Samuel 3:10).

—*Rose From Brier*

Questions to Consider

1. Do you feel as though you're sinking today? In what way?

2. Listen carefully. What might God be immediately saying to you?

A Prayerful Response

Lord, I will immediately call on You when I'm beginning to sink. Amen.

Blow upon My Garden

Thought for Today

The winds of spiritual adversity can blow God's fragrance upon you.

Wisdom from Scripture

I waited patiently for the LORD; he turned to me and heard my cry.

He lifted me out of the slimy pit, out of the mud and mire; he set my feet on a rock and gave me a firm place to stand. He put a new song in my mouth, a hymn of praise to our God. Many will see and fear and put their trust in the LORD.

Blessed is the man who makes the LORD his trust, who does not look to the proud, to those who turn aside to false gods.

Many, O LORD my God, are the wonders you have done. The things you planned for us no one can recount to you; were I to speak and tell of them, they would be too many to declare.

Sacrifice and offering you did not desire, but my ears you have pierced; burnt offerings and sin offerings you did not require.

Then I said, "Here I am, I have come—it is written about me in the scroll. I desire to do your will, O my God; your law is within my heart."

I proclaim righteousness in the great assembly; I do not seal my lips, as you know, O LORD. I do not hide your righteousness in my heart; I speak of your faithfulness and salvation. I do not conceal your love and your truth from the great assembly.

Do not withhold your mercy from me, O LORD; may your

love and your truth always protect me. For troubles without number surround me; my sins have overtaken me, and I cannot see. They are more than the hairs of my head, and my heart fails within me.

Be pleased, O LORD, to save me; O LORD, come quickly to help me.

May all who seek to take my life be put to shame and confusion; may all who desire my ruin be turned back in disgrace. May those who say to me, "Aha! Aha!" be appalled at their own shame.

But may all who seek you rejoice and be glad in you; may those who love your salvation always say, "The LORD be exalted!"

Yet I am poor and needy; may the Lord think of me. You are my help and my deliverer; O my God, do not delay.

PSALM 40, NIV

INSIGHTS FROM AMY CARMICHAEL

Long ago a child, wedged in between three grownups on a sofa, listened, astonished, to one of those great people questioning the rightness of a certain prayer in a hymn.

"I do not think we should pray, 'Send grief and pain,'" remarked this audacious Irishwoman. It was quite wrong, of course, for was not a hymnbook almost as inspired as the Bible?

But the day came when the child understood. It is only those who have never tasted real grief, real pain, who would dare to pray like that. Nor would anyone who had endured anything worth calling pain call it "sweet." ("Sweet are Thy messengers, sweet their refrain," says the hymn. St. Paul called his thorn the messenger of Satan.)

To suffer intensely in soul or in body is to see pain for what it is: a dominating and fearful thing. You do not try to penetrate its mystery; you are far too tired to do anything of the kind. Nor do you at that moment exult. We do not read of our Lord exulting in bodily agony. Yet, because for eternal reasons pain was bound up with the fulfillment of His Father's will, He could say without a shadow of reservation, "I delight to do Thy will, O my God: yea, Thy law is within my heart" (Psalms 40:8).

Through the garden the north wind is blowing now. Receive it, O my soul. All sharpness, all hardness, the difficult, the undesired; refuse none of these things. Set the doors into the secret avenues of being wide open to north wind or to south.

In Southern India the wind is often hot, and hot air rises like a burning breath from the ground. Such a wind parches the spirit, drains it of vitality, sends it to seek some cool place, caring only to find a shadow from the heat.

But be the wind scorching, or sharp and cold, it can only cause the spices of His garden to flow out. And often, have we not found it so? The Lord of the garden calls His south wind; and all the flowers know it is blowing, and are glad.   —*Rose From Brier*

QUESTIONS TO CONSIDER

1. What does Jesus' example teach you about "delighting" in God's will?

2. In what ways can you exude God's fragrance as the winds of adversity blow?

A PRAYERFUL RESPONSE

Lord, I want to be like Jesus who delighted to do Your will. Please show me how. Amen.

DAY 6

OUR EVERYDAY GOD

THOUGHT FOR TODAY

Even during small and ordinary annoyances, God is with you.

WISDOM FROM SCRIPTURE

May God arise, may his enemies be scattered; may his foes flee before him.

As smoke is blown away by the wind, may you blow them away; as wax melts before the fire, may the wicked perish before God. But may the righteous be glad and rejoice before God; may they be happy and joyful.

Sing to God, sing praise to his name, extol him who rides on the clouds—his name is the LORD—and rejoice before him.

A father to the fatherless, a defender of widows, is God in his holy dwelling. God sets the lonely in families, he leads forth the prisoners with singing; but the rebellious live in a sun-scorched land.

When you went out before your people, O God, when you marched through the wasteland, the earth shook, the heavens poured down rain, before God, the One of Sinai, before God, the God of Israel.

You gave abundant showers, O God; you refreshed your weary inheritance. Your people settled in it, and from your bounty, O God, you provided for the poor.

The LORD announced the word, and great was the company of those who proclaimed it: "Kings and armies flee in haste; in the camps men divide the plunder.

"Even while you sleep among the campfires, the wings of

my dove are sheathed with silver, its feathers with shining gold."

When the Almighty scattered the kings in the land, it was like snow fallen on Zalmon. The mountains of Bashan are majestic mountains; rugged are the mountains of Bashan.

Why gaze in envy, O rugged mountains, at the mountain where God chooses to reign, where the LORD himself will dwell forever?

The chariots of God are tens of thousands and thousands of thousands; the Lord has come from Sinai into his sanctuary. When you ascended on high, you led captives in your train; you received gifts from men, even from the rebellious—that you, O LORD God, might dwell there.

Praise be to the Lord, to God our Savior, who daily bears our burdens.   PSALMS 68:1-19, NIV

INSIGHTS FROM AMY CARMICHAEL

The best training is to learn to accept everything as it comes, as from Him whom our soul loves. The tests are always unexpected things, not great things that can be written up, but the common little rubs of life, silly little nothings, things you are ashamed of minding one scrap. Yet they can knock a strong person over and lay him low.

It is a good thing to learn to take these things by the right handle. An inward grouse is a devastating thing. I expect you know this, we all do; but it is extraordinary how the devil tries to "get" us on the ordinary road of life. But all is well if we are deep in Him, and He in us, our daily strength and joy and song.

I have read and reread about the love that constrains. Nothing less will hold on to the end. Feelings can be shaken and fight can be fearfully discouraging, for sometimes we seem to be losing ground and all seems to be going wrong. Then the devil comes and paints glorious pictures of what might have been. He did to me; I can see those pictures still. But as we go on steadfastly obeying the word that compelled, we do become aware that it is all worthwhile. We *know* it, we *know* Him with us, and that is life.

I ask that the consciousness of His presence with you may be constant and sweet. I know the difference this makes.

But you are not a child in Him; you have passed the point where that is needful. You *know* Him near, with you and in you. Joy though it is to be conscious of that blessed One, the great thing is not your feeling, but His fact. So if there are fogs on the sea on any day or night—still all is well.   —*Candles in the Dark*

Questions to Consider

1. Think of times when you have experienced God's presence in the "common little rubs" of life. What difference did it make?

2. How can you keep the devil from "getting" you during life's ordinary moments?

A Prayerful Response

Lord, I ask for the assurance of Your presence in my life. Thank You. Amen.

33

PART TWO

THE GOD OF ALL COMFORT

A great wind blowing, raging sea,
And rowers toiling wearily,
Far from the land where they would be.

And then One coming, drawing nigh;
They care not now for starless sky.
The Light of life says It is I.

They care not now for toil of oar,
For lo, the ship is at the shore,
And their Beloved they adore.

Lord of the Lake of Galilee,
Who long ago walked on the sea,
My heart is comforted in Thee.

"COMFORTED," *TOWARD JERUSALEM*

AMY CARMICHAEL'S INSIGHT

When the winds of difficulty blow and batter your world,
you can run to God as a safe place to hide
and a very present help during trouble.

THE COMFORT OF THY HELP AGAIN

THOUGHT FOR TODAY

God revives and restores the weary soul.

WISDOM FROM SCRIPTURE

In you, O LORD, I take refuge; let me never be put to shame.

In your righteousness deliver me and rescue me; incline your ear to me and save me. Be to me a rock of refuge, a strong fortress, to save me, for you are my rock and my fortress.

Rescue me, O my God, from the hand of the wicked, from the grasp of the unjust and cruel. For you, O LORD, are my hope, my trust, O LORD, from my youth.

Upon you I have leaned from my birth; it was you who took me from my mother's womb. My praise is continually of you.

I have been like a portent to many, but you are my strong refuge.

My mouth is filled with your praise, and with your glory all day long.

Do not cast me off in the time of old age; do not forsake me when my strength is spent. For my enemies speak concerning me, and those who watch for my life consult together.

They say, "Pursue and seize that person whom God has forsaken, for there is no one to deliver."

O God, do not be far from me; O my God, make haste to

help me! Let my accusers be put to shame and consumed; let those who seek to hurt me be covered with scorn and disgrace.

But I will hope continually, and will praise you yet more and more.

My mouth will tell of your righteous acts, of your deeds of salvation all day long, though their number is past my knowledge. I will come praising the mighty deeds of the LORD GOD, I will praise your righteousness, yours alone.

O God, from my youth you have taught me, and I still proclaim your wondrous deeds.

So even to old age and gray hairs, O God, do not forsake me, until I proclaim your might to all the generations to come. Your power and your righteousness, O God, reach the high heavens. You who have done great things, O God, who is like you?

You who have made me see many troubles and calamities will revive me again; from the depths of the earth you will bring me up again. You will increase my honor, and comfort me once again.   PSALMS 71:1-21, RSV

INSIGHTS FROM AMY CARMICHAEL

Note: Amy based this essay on a photo of a frost-bound tree.

"I was a tall young tree. And many a forest creature and bird found succour in my strength and comfort under my leaves, for they made me a wide, cool shadow, like the shadow of a great rock in a weary land.

"But now it is not so. It seems as if it could never be so any more. Frost-bound I stand. I can endure, for I have asked for fortitude, and I trust that I have not asked in vain. But I cannot do what I once did. My sap is frozen within me and no bird builds her nest in my cold boughs—those happy birds that sang among my branches, where are they now? O that I had done more for them when power to do was mine!

"And I am not alone in this cold solitude; I am only one of many. Those others, frozen as I am, stand as I stand today. Our green days are past; our purposes are broken off, even the thoughts of our hearts.

"O give me the comfort of Thy help again, my God, and bring my soul out of prison, that I may praise Thy name. There is forgiveness with Thee; unto Thee, O Lord, do I lift up my soul. Hear my voice according to Thy loving-kindness: revive me, O Lord, according to thy loving-kindness. Look Thou unto me, and be merciful to me, as Thou doest unto those that love Thy name.

"The words of men cannot help me now: miserable comforters are they all. Speak Thou to me, O God, for with Thee is the fountain of life. Let Thy tender mercies come unto me that I may live. O God, be not far from me. O my Strength, hasten to help me."

"My child, thou hast made thy prayer unto Me in an acceptable time. In the multitude of My mercy I have heard thee; in the truth of My salvation I have delivered thee. O cast thy burden upon the Lord, and He shall sustain thee. It is He that hath made Summer and Winter."

"Summer and Winter? Then Thou hast not shut me up into the hand of the enemy. I had thought that I and those others were so shut up in this prison of frost that we could not come forth."

"But my frost-bound ones are the bond servants of their Lord. My mercy encompasses them. Every part of thy being is embraced

in the shining of My mercy. Thou hast said in thine heart, 'All these things are against me,' but one day thou shalt say, 'Blessed be morsels of ice, hail, snow, and vapors.' Thou shalt know that all these things were fulfilling My word."

"I know it now. From Thee came the ice and the hoary frost of heaven. My life was as the face of the deep when it is frozen, but Thou has given me grace to help in time of need. I will trust, and not be afraid. Blessed be God who hath not turned away my prayer, nor His mercy from me. The day is Thine, the night also is Thine; Thou hast prepared the light and the sun, Thou hast set all the borders of the earth. Thou hast made Summer and Winter. My times are in Thy hand. Thy word hath revived me."

For a little while he was silent and then he said to his God, "I will fear no evil, for Thou art with me" (Psalms 23:4).

And his God answered him in words whose depths no one has sounded, *"I will never leave thee or forsake thee"* (Hebrews 13:5).   —*Figures of the True*

Questions to Consider

1. In what ways can you relate to the frost-bound tree's lament?

2. What comfort can you find in God, despite your circumstances?

A Prayerful Response

Lord, please grant me daily refuge so I can take comfort in You. Amen.

A Firm Grasp of the Hand

Thought for Today

God asks you to lean on Him instead of others, or even yourself.

Wisdom from Scripture

My child, do not forget my teaching, but let your heart keep my commandments; for length of days and years of life and abundant welfare they will give you.

Do not let loyalty and faithfulness forsake you; bind them around your neck, write them on the tablet of your heart. So you will find favor and good repute in the sight of God and of people.

Trust in the LORD with all your heart, and do not rely on your own insight. In all your ways acknowledge him, and he will make straight your paths.

Do not be wise in your own eyes; fear the LORD, and turn away from evil. It will be a healing for your flesh and a refreshment for your body.

O Most High, when I am afraid, I put my trust in you. In God, whose word I praise, in God I trust; I am not afraid; what can flesh do to me?

All day long they seek to injure my cause; all their thoughts are against me for evil. They stir up strife, they lurk, they watch my steps. As they hoped to have my life, so repay them for their crime; in wrath cast down the peoples, O God!

You have kept count of my tossings; put my tears in your

bottle. Are they not in your record? Then my enemies will retreat in the day when I call. This I know, that God is for me.

In God, whose word I praise, in the LORD, whose word I praise, in God I trust; I am not afraid. What can a mere mortal do to me?

My vows to you I must perform, O God; I will render thank offerings to you. For you have delivered my soul from death, and my feet from falling, so that I may walk before God in the light of life.

PROVERBS 3:1-8; PSALMS 56:2-13, RSV

INSIGHTS FROM AMY CARMICHAEL

Thus spake Jehovah unto me like a firm grasp of the hand.

ISAIAH 8:11, ROTHERHAM

Blessed be the Lord our God who causes His word to come to us this way.

Sometimes this firm grasp comes through deepened insight into a single word. It has come to me through the word "trust," which I find in Young means to *lean on—trust—confide*. I found that Rotherham sometimes translates it *lean on* as in, "On Thee do we lean" (2 Chronicles 14:11), and "Because thou has not leaned" (2 Chronicles 16:7).

"I have trusted in Thy mercy [*leaned on* Thy mercy]" (Psalms 13:5), that mercy which has loved us with an everlasting love, which pardons and cleanses and will never tire of us.

"He that trusteth in the Lord [*leaneth* on the Lord], mercy shall compass him about" (Psalms 32:10).

Is it not like Him to let us know that He wants us to lean, not only on His mercy, but on His very Self?

"Now there was *leaning* on Jesus' bosom one of His disciples, whom Jesus loved" (John 13:23). It was when John was leaning, that he heard his Lord's answer to a question which puzzled the others.

"Whoso *leaneth* on the Lord, happy is he" (Proverbs 16:20). He is indeed.

The same verb is used in some of the verses that are never far from us, such as, "Cause me to hear... for on Thee do I *lean*" (Psalms 143:8).

"What time I am afraid, I will *lean* on Thee" (Psalms 56:3).

"I will *lean,* and not be afraid" (Isaiah 12:2).

"Thou wilt keep him in perfect peace... because he *leaneth* on Thee.... *Lean ye* on the Lord forever: for in the Lord Jehovah is everlasting strength" (Isaiah 26:3-4).

Can we wonder that the blessed Spirit, who guides in the choice of words, led the writer who was longing to tell of the delight of answered prayer to this special verb, which so clearly shows that nothing in us accounts for the Lord's goodness to us? It is all, all of Him.

"The Lord is my strength and my shield; my heart *leaned on* Him, and I am helped: therefore my heart greatly rejoiceth; and with my song I will praise Him" (Psalms 28:7).

May the Lord of love make this word of His to be "like a firm grasp of the hand" to teach each one of us.

—*Thou Givest... They Gather*

43

Questions to Consider

1. Is it difficult for you to lean on God rather than on others or yourself? Why or why not?

2. When you have leaned on God, what were the results?

A Prayerful Response

Lord, I trust in You and will not lean on my own understanding. Amen.

A Rose from Brier

Thought for Today

God wants you to find contentment in Him alone.

Wisdom from Scripture

O give thanks to the LORD, for he is good; his steadfast love endures forever!

Let Israel say, "His steadfast love endures forever." Let the house of Aaron say, "His steadfast love endures forever." Let those who fear the LORD say, "His steadfast love endures forever."

Out of my distress I called on the LORD; the LORD answered me and set me in a broad place.

With the LORD on my side I do not fear. What can mortals do to me? The LORD is on my side to help me; I shall look in triumph on those who hate me.

It is better to take refuge in the LORD than to put confidence in mortals. It is better to take refuge in the LORD than to put confidence in princes.

Open to me the gates of righteousness, that I may enter through them and give thanks to the LORD. This is the gate of the LORD; the righteous shall enter through it.

I thank you that you have answered me and have become my salvation.

The stone that the builders rejected has become the chief cornerstone. This is the LORD's doing; it is marvelous in our eyes.

This is the day that the LORD has made; let us rejoice and be glad in it.

Save us, we beseech you, O LORD! O LORD, we beseech you, give us success!

Blessed is the one who comes in the name of the LORD. We bless you from the house of the LORD.

The LORD is God, and he has given us light. Bind the festal procession with branches, up to the horns of the altar.

You are my God, and I will give thanks to you; you are my God, I will extol you. O give thanks to the LORD, for he is good, for his steadfast love endures forever.

PSALMS 118:1-9; 19-29, RSV

INSIGHTS FROM AMY CARMICHAEL

"I have no desire for my imprisonment to end before the right time; I love my chains. My senses, indeed, have not any relish for such things, but my heart is separated from them and borne over them."

Madame Guyon said that. I cannot say that I love my chains in any literal sense, nor do I feel that we are meant to do so. Our Lord did not tell the woman who was bound to love the cords that bound her. But in the sense that I am sure Madame Guyon meant the words (for, she said, her senses had no relish for such things) I believe He can help us to find something truly lovable in that which is His will for us.

For example, disappointments. In quiet procession these weary little things have entered this room. After my foot began to mend other troubles came, one after the other, pulling me down just when it seemed as though I might soon begin to walk. As each corner was turned we thought it would be the last, but there was always another.

But one of the first of these disappointments was lightened by something sweet and dear. One of our fellowship was at home on furlough, and he was to return to us on February 25. I had set my heart on being up and ready to meet him and the new brother whom he was bringing with him. I was sure I could be at the welcome service when that song was to be sung. For a month or so before that date it had seemed that this would be. Then the hope gradually faded. I was still in bed when they came, not even in a chair.

That morning, while the chiming bells of welcome were being rung from the tower, I was far more in the midst of that beloved crowd in the house of prayer than here. And I ached to be there really, not just in spirit—ached till everything was one ache. And then, each word as clear as though it slid down the chiming bells, this little song came to me:

Thou has not *that*, My child, but Thou hast Me,
And am not I alone enough for thee?
I know it all, know how thy heart was set
Upon this joy which is not given yet.

And well I know how much through the wistful days
Thou walkest all the dear familiar ways,
As unregarded as a breath of air,
But there in love and longing, always there.

I know it all; but from thy brier shall blow
A rose for others. If it were not so,
I would have told thee. Come, then, say to Me,
My Lord, My Lord, I am content with thee.

"From thy brier shall blow a rose for others." In the hills of South India there are tall and beautiful bushes of wild roses. The roses are larger than ours at home and of an unforgettable sweetness. But they were not called to mind then by these words. I saw instead a little, low, very prickly bush in an old-fashioned English garden; it was covered with inconspicuous pink roses. But the wonder of the bush was its all-pervading fragrance, for it was a sweetbrier.

I think that when He whom our soul loves comes so near to us, and so gently helps our human weaknesses, then what Madame Guyon wrote nearly three hundred years ago becomes a present truth. We are borne over the oppression that would hold us down, we mount up on wings, we find a secret sweetness in our brier. But it is not of us. It is Love that lifts us up. It is Love that is the sweetness.

Is the one who reads this in a great weariness, or in the exhaustion that follows a sore hurt, or in the terrible grasp of pain? He who loves as no one else can love, who understands to the uttermost, is not far away. He wants us to say, He can help us to say, "My Lord, my Love, I am content with Thee."

—*Rose From Brier*

QUESTIONS TO CONSIDER

1. What do you want that you do not have?

2. Why would God want you to be content with Him alone?

A PRAYERFUL RESPONSE

Lord, I want to find contentment in You alone. I ask for Your understanding as I journey toward this goal. Amen.

A Very Present Help

Thought for Today

When you call on Him, God is "a very present help" during difficulty.

Wisdom from Scripture

God is our refuge and strength, a very present help in trouble.

Therefore we will not fear, though the earth should change, though the mountains shake in the heart of the sea; though its waters roar and foam, though the mountains tremble with its tumult.

There is a river whose streams make glad the city of God, the holy habitation of the Most High. God is in the midst of the city; it shall not be moved; God will help it when the morning dawns.

The nations are in an uproar, the kingdoms totter; he utters his voice, the earth melts. The LORD of hosts is with us; the God of Jacob is our refuge.

Come, behold the works of the LORD; see what desolations he has brought on the earth. He makes wars cease to the end of the earth; he breaks the bow, and shatters the spear; he burns the shields with fire.

"Be still, and know that I am God! I am exalted among the nations, I am exalted in the earth."

The LORD of hosts is with us; the God of Jacob is our refuge.

PSALM 46, RSV

Which is harder: to do or to endure?

I think to endure is much harder, and our Father loves us too much to let us pass through life without learning to endure. So I want you to welcome the difficult little things, the tiny pricks and ruffles that are sure to come almost every day. For they give you a chance to say "No" to yourself, and by doing so you will become strong not only to do but also to endure.

Whatever happens, don't be sorry for yourselves. You know how our Lord met the tempting "Pity Thyself" (Matthew 16:22, Authorized Version margin). After all, what is anything we have to bear in comparison with what our Lord bore for us?

I know that each one of you is in need of continual help if you are continually to conquer. I have splendid words to give you; they are from the first verse of Psalm 46: *"A very present help."*

Our loving Lord is not just present, but nearer than thought can imagine—so near that a whisper can reach Him. You know the story of the man who had a quick temper and had no time to go away and pray for help. His habit was to send up a little telegraph prayer—"Thy sweetness, Lord!"—and sweetness came.

Do you need courage? "Thy courage, Lord!" Patience? "Thy patience, Lord!" Love? "Thy love, Lord!" A quiet mind? "Thy quietness, Lord!"

Shall we all practice this swift and simple way of prayer more and more? If we do, our Very Present Help will not disappoint us. For Thou, Lord, hast never failed them that seek Thee.

—Candles in the Dark

Questions to Consider

1. What need of yours often requires God's "very present help"?

2. When this need arises, how can you practice Amy's "simple way of prayer"?

A Prayerful Response

Lord, please be my "very present help" when I call on You. Open my spiritual eyes to recognize Your response. Amen.

THE ANGEL CAME THE SECOND TIME

THOUGHT FOR TODAY

God will repeatedly refresh and remind you that He has overcome the world.

WISDOM FROM SCRIPTURE

Ahab told Jezebel all that Elijah had done, and how he had killed all the prophets with the sword.

Then Jezebel sent a messenger to Elijah, saying, "So may the gods do to me, and more also, if I do not make your life like the life of one of them by this time tomorrow."

Then he was afraid; he got up and fled for his life, and came to Beer-sheba, which belongs to Judah; he left his servant there.

But he himself went a day's journey into the wilderness, and came and sat down under a solitary broom tree. He asked that he might die: "It is enough; now, O LORD, take away my life, for I am no better than my ancestors."

Then he lay down under the broom tree and fell asleep. Suddenly an angel touched him and said to him, "Get up and eat."

He looked, and there at his head was a cake baked on hot stones, and a jar of water. He ate and drank, and lay down again.

The angel of the LORD came a second time, touched him, and said, "Get up and eat, otherwise the journey will be too much for you."

He got up, and ate and drank; then he went in the

strength of that food forty days and forty nights to Horeb the mount of God. 1 KINGS 19:1-8, RSV

INSIGHTS FROM AMY CARMICHAEL

I have told how it came to be a custom to share my pot of manna in the form of a short note. I did not know till lately that some had copied these notes from day to day. To turn over the leaves of such a notebook is like turning back the weeks and months and looking at the past days again. This is what I find soon after the comforting assurance came, "Upon thy brier shall blow a rose for others."

Is it not good and comforting to know that the angel of the Lord came again the second time? We never reach the place where we pass beyond the compassion of our God: His compassions fail not; they are new every morning; never tiring of us, always strong for our help.

There have been times for nearly all of us when we have felt the truth of the angel's word, "The journey is too great for thee"; but have we not always found the Bread of Life and the Water of Life ready for our sustenance? And in the strength of that meat we have gone on, and shall go on, even unto the Mount of God.

But the perplexing thing is that even after we have been comforted and strengthened we can feel quite weak and tired again, just as though we had never been fed on the blessed Cake of Bread, the Water turned to Wine. It is consoling to find that we are not alone there.

That heavenly minded book, *Revelations of Divine Love,* which has opened to me more than ever during these months, is refreshingly candid. After Julian of Norwich had seen the fifteen Shewings [revelations from God] that, falling far and steadily, each following the other, had gladdened her heart, she wrote:

And at the end all was close [hidden], and I saw no more. And soon I felt that I should live and languish; and soon my sickness came again: first in my head with a sound and a din, and suddenly all my body was fulfilled with sickness as it was before. And I was as barren and as dry as if I never had comfort but little.

But her courteous Lord did not leave her; the words of solace follow a little later: "*Thou shalt not be overcome*" was said clearly and mightily, for assurance and comfort against all tribulations that may come. He said not: "*Thou shalt not be tempested, thou shalt not be travailed, thou shalt not be afflicted.*" But He said: "*Thou shalt not be overcome.*"

God willeth that we take heed to these words, and that we be ever strong in sure trust, in weal and woe. For He loveth and enjoyeth us, and so willeth He that we love and enjoy Him and mightily trust in Him; and all shall be well.

Blessed be the patience of our Lord, our dear-worthy Redeemer. The angel of the Lord came again the second time.

—*Rose From Brier*

QUESTIONS TO CONSIDER

1. Do you need God to visit you a second time regarding a particular problem that leaves you weak and tired?

2. What might Jesus' words, "Thou shalt not be overcome" mean in your situation?

A Prayerful Response

Lord, nourish my soul with the reminder that You have overcome the world. Amen.

GRACE FOR GRACE

THOUGHT FOR TODAY

God's grace covers all of your failures: past, present, and future.

WISDOM FROM SCRIPTURE

Therefore, since we are justified by faith, we have peace with God through our Lord Jesus Christ, through whom we have obtained access to this grace in which we stand; and we boast in our hope of sharing the glory of God.

And not only that, but we also boast in our sufferings, knowing that suffering produces endurance, and endurance produces character, and character produces hope, and hope does not disappoint us, because God's love has been poured into our hearts through the Holy Spirit that has been given to us.

For while we were still weak, at the right time Christ died for the ungodly. Indeed, rarely will anyone die for a righteous person—though perhaps for a good person someone might actually dare to die.

But God proves his love for us in that while we still were sinners Christ died for us. Much more surely then, now that we have been justified by his blood, will we be saved through him from the wrath of God.

For if while we were enemies, we were reconciled to God through the death of his Son, much more surely, having been reconciled, will we be saved by his life. But more than that, we even boast in God through our Lord Jesus Christ, through whom we have now received reconciliation.

What then are we to say? Should we continue in sin in order that grace may abound?

By no means! How can we who died to sin go on living in it?

Do you not know that all of us who have been baptized into Christ Jesus were baptized into his death?

Therefore we have been buried with him by baptism into death, so that, just as Christ was raised from the dead by the glory of the Father, so we too might walk in newness of life.

So you also must consider yourselves dead to sin and alive to God in Christ Jesus. Therefore, do not let sin exercise dominion in your mortal bodies, to make you obey their passions.

No longer present your members to sin as instruments of wickedness, but present yourselves to God as those who have been brought from death to life, and present your members to God as instruments of righteousness.

For sin will have no dominion over you, since you are not under law but under grace.

ROMANS 5:1-11; 6:1-4, 11-14, RSV

INSIGHTS FROM AMY CARMICHAEL

Sometimes, when we are distressed by past failure and tormented by fear of failure in the future, nothing helps so much as to give some familiar Scripture time to enter into us and become part of our being.

The words "grace for grace" have been a help to me since I read in a little old book of Bishop Moule's something that opened their meaning. (Till then I had not understood them.) He says "for" means simply "instead."

The image is of a perpetual success of supply; a displacement ever going on; ceaseless change of need and demand.

The picture before us is of a river. Stand on its banks, and contemplate the flow of waters. A minute passes, and another. Is it the same stream still? Yes. But is it the same water? No. The liquid mass that passed you a few seconds ago now fills another section of the channel; new water has displaced it, or if you please, replaced it. *Water instead of water.*

And so hour by hour, and year by year, and century by century, the process holds: one stream, other waters—living, not stagnant, because always in the great identity there is perpetual exchange. Grace takes the place of grace [and love takes the place of love]; ever new, ever old, ever the same, ever fresh and young, for hour by hour, for year by year, through Christ.   —*If*

QUESTIONS TO CONSIDER

1. What does "grace" mean to you?

2. In what situation do you need a perpetual supply of God's grace? How can you allow His grace to flow through you?

A PRAYERFUL RESPONSE

Lord, I accept Your ever-flowing grace and thank You for it. Amen.

GIVE TIME TO QUIETNESS

THOUGHT FOR TODAY

Devoting time to quietness opens your ears and heart to God's voice.

WISDOM FROM SCRIPTURE

The LORD is my light and my salvation; whom shall I fear? The LORD is the stronghold of my life; of whom shall I be afraid?

When evildoers assail me to devour my flesh—my adversaries and foes—they shall stumble and fall. Though an army encamp against me, my heart shall not fear; though war rise up against me, yet I will be confident.

One thing I asked of the LORD, that will I seek after: to live in the house of the LORD all the days of my life, to behold the beauty of the LORD, and to inquire in his temple.

For he will hide me in his shelter in the day of trouble; he will conceal me under the cover of his tent; he will set me high on a rock.

Now my head is lifted up above my enemies all around me, and I will offer in his tent sacrifices with shouts of joy; I will sing and make melody to the LORD.

Hear, O LORD, when I cry aloud, be gracious to me and answer me!

"Come," my heart says, "seek his face!" Your face, LORD, do I seek.

Do not hide your face from me. Do not turn your servant away in anger, you who have been my help. Do not cast me off, do not forsake me, O God of my salvation!

If my father and mother forsake me, the LORD will take me up.

Teach me your way, O LORD, and lead me on a level path because of my enemies. Do not give me up to the will of my adversaries, for false witnesses have risen against me, and they are breathing out violence.

I believe that I shall see the goodness of the LORD in the land of the living.

Wait for the LORD; be strong, and let your heart take courage; wait for the LORD!   PSALM 27, RSV

INSIGHTS FROM AMY CARMICHAEL

The fight to which we have been called is not an easy fight. We are touching the very center of the devil's power and kingdom, and he hates us intensely and fights hard against us. We have no chance at all of winning in this fight unless we are disciplined soldiers, utterly out-and-out and uncompromising, and men and women of prayer.

So first, give much time to quietness. For the most part we have to get our help directly from our God. We are here to help, not to be helped, and we must each learn to walk with God alone and feed on His Word so as to be nourished. Don't only read and pray; *listen*. And don't evade the slightest whisper of guidance that comes. May God make you very sensitive, and very obedient.

Fill up the crevices of time with the things that matter most. This will cost something, but it is worth it. "Seek ye My face. My heart said unto Thee, Thy face, Lord, will I seek" (Psalms

27:8). No one is of much use who does not truly want to learn what it means to pray and listen and definitively choose the life that is hid with Christ in God.

Keep close, keep close. If you are close you will be keen. Your heart will be set on the things that abide. You will drink of His Spirit and you will thirst for souls even as He thirsts. You will not be attracted by the world that crucified Him, but you will love the people in that world who have never seen His beauty and are losing so much more than they know. You will live to share your joy in Him. Nothing else will count for much.

All this will be, if you walk with Him as with a visible Companion, from dawn through all the hours till you go to sleep at night. And your nights will be holy too, for He is watching over your sleep as your mother watched over it when you were a tiny child.   —*Candles in the Dark*

Questions to Consider

1. How can you arrange time for quietness?

2. If you "keep close" to God, what evidence of His presence will materialize in your life?

A Prayerful Response

Lord, I will come to You in quietness, listening for Your words to me. Amen.

BE STRONG, BE STRONG

THOUGHT FOR TODAY

True comfort strengthens you emotionally and spiritually.

WISDOM FROM SCRIPTURE

Finally, be strong in the Lord and in the strength of his power.

Put on the whole armor of God, so that you may be able to stand against the wiles of the devil.

For our struggle is not against enemies of blood and flesh, but against the rulers, against the authorities, against the cosmic powers of this present darkness, against the spiritual forces of evil in the heavenly places.

Therefore take up the whole armor of God, so that you may be able to withstand on that evil day, and having done everything, to stand firm.

Stand therefore, and fasten the belt of truth around your waist, and put on the breastplate of righteousness. As shoes for your feet put on whatever will make you ready to proclaim the gospel of peace.

With all of these, take the shield of faith, with which you will be able to quench all the flaming arrows of the evil one. Take the helmet of salvation, and the sword of the Spirit, which is the word of God.

Pray in the Spirit at all times in every prayer and supplication. To that end keep alert and always persevere in supplication for all the saints.   EPHESIANS 6:10-18, RSV

INSIGHTS FROM AMY CARMICHAEL

Many think of comfort as if it were a gentle kind of soothing and nothing else. But the Oxford Dictionary gives its derivation, *con fortare*. So "to strengthen" is its first meaning. And it has been explained beautifully, I think, as "to raise up from depression."

I have heard one who was (she thought) comforting another say, "How hard it is for you." But that sort of talk does not raise up, it pushes down. It is weakening, not strengthening.

God's comfort is never weakening. He leaves the soul He comforts stronger to fight, braver to suffer, grateful, not sorry for itself, keen to go on "to strive, to seek, to find, and not to yield."

At the completion of the reading of any of the books of Moses in the synagogue, it was the custom for the congregation to exclaim, "Be strong, be strong, and let us strengthen one another!" In like manner, when we see others under the enemy's attack, let us brace and strengthen them.

God make us all comforters in that strong sense of the word—His fellow-comforters.

Someone has said:

What we can suffer for another is the test of love;
What we can do for another is the test of power.
God, let me be aware;
Stab my soul fiercely with another's pain;
Let me walk, seeing horror and stain;
Let my hands, groping, find other hands;
Give me the heart that divines and understands;
Give me courage, wounded, to fight;
Flood me with knowledge, drench me with light.

—Thou Givest... They Gather

QUESTIONS TO CONSIDER

1. What is the worst "comfort" you've received? The best?

2. How can you give and receive comfort that strengthens the soul?

A PRAYERFUL RESPONSE

Lord, teach me to comfort others as You comfort and strengthen me. Amen.

PART THREE

THE FELLOWSHIP OF HIS SUFFERINGS

Hast thou no scar?
No hidden scar on foot, or side, or hand?
I hear thee sung as mighty in the land,
I hear them hail thy bright ascendant star,
Hast thou no scar?

Hast thou no wound?
Yet I was wounded by the archers, spent,
Leaned Me against a tree to die; and rent
By ravening beasts that compassed Me, I swooned:
Hast thou no wound?

No wound? no scar?
Yet, as the Master shall the servant be,
And pierced are the feet that follow Me;
But thine are whole: can he have followed far
Who has no wound nor scar?

"NO SCAR?" *TOWARD JERUSALEM*

AMY CARMICHAEL'S INSIGHT

When you enter the fellowship of Christ's sufferings,
you can become more like Him.

CLIMBING HIGHER

THOUGHT FOR TODAY

God asks His children to climb higher spiritually and personally.

WISDOM FROM SCRIPTURE

I love you, O LORD, my strength.

The LORD is my rock, my fortress and my deliverer; my God is my rock, in whom I take refuge. He is my shield and the horn of my salvation, my stronghold.

I call to the LORD, who is worthy of praise, and I am saved from my enemies.

He reached down from on high and took hold of me; he drew me out of deep waters. He rescued me from my powerful enemy, from my foes, who were too strong for me. They confronted me in the day of my disaster, but the LORD was my support.

He brought me out into a spacious place; he rescued me because he delighted in me.

The LORD has dealt with me according to my righteousness; according to the cleanness of my hands he has rewarded me. For I have kept the ways of the LORD; I have not done evil by turning from my God.

All his laws are before me; I have not turned away from his decrees. I have been blameless before him and have kept myself from sin.

The LORD has rewarded me according to my righteousness, according to the cleanness of my hands in his sight.

To the faithful you show yourself faithful, to the blameless you show yourself blameless, to the pure you show yourself pure, but to the crooked you show yourself shrewd.

You save the humble but bring low those whose eyes are haughty. You, O LORD, keep my lamp burning; my God turns my darkness into light. With your help I can advance against a troop; with my God I can scale a wall.

As for God, his way is perfect; the word of the LORD is flawless. He is a shield for all who take refuge in him. For who is God besides the LORD? And who is the Rock except our God?

It is God who arms me with strength and makes my way perfect. He makes my feet like the feet of a deer; he enables me to stand on the heights. He trains my hands for battle; my arms can bend a bow of bronze.

You give me your shield of victory, and your right hand sustains me; you stoop down to make me great. You broaden the path beneath me, so that my ankles do not turn.

PSALMS 18:1-3, 16-36, NIV

INSIGHTS FROM AMY CARMICHAEL

A voice said, *"Climb."* And he said, "How shall I climb? The mountains are so steep that I cannot climb."

The voice said, *"Climb or die."*

He said, "But how? I see no way up those steep ascents. This that is asked of me is too hard for me."

The voice said, "Climb or perish, soul and body of thee, mind and spirit of thee. There is no second choice for any son of man. *Climb or die.*"

Then he remembered that he had read in the books of the

bravest climbers on the hills of earth, that sometimes they were aware of the presence of a Companion on the mountains who was not one of the earthly party of climbers. How much more certain was the presence of his Guide as he climbed the high places of the spirit.

And he remembered a word in the *Book of Mountaineers* that heartened him: *My soul is continually in my hand* (Psalms 119:109). It heartened him, for it told him that he was created to walk in precarious places, not on the easy levels of life.

This decision that had to be made, this stern task that would test the fiber of character, this duty that must be performed, this blame that must be accepted without self-defense or resentment—these things were part of the day's work for the true mountaineer. And he said to his foe, Love-of-fleshly-ease, "Rejoice not against me, O mine enemy: when I fall, I shall arise; when I sit in darkness, the Lord shall be a light unto me. I will go in the strength of the Lord God" (Micah 7:8).

And other words came and put new life into him: "When I said, my foot slippeth; Thy mercy, O Lord, held me upon my high places. Thou hast enlarged my steps under me, that my feet did not slip. Thou hast girded me with strength. Hold Thou me up and I shall be safe" (Psalms 94:18; 18:36, 39; 119:17).

And he said, *"I will climb."*   —*Figures of the True*

QUESTIONS TO CONSIDER

1. How might God be asking you to climb higher, either spiritually or personally?

2. Why do you think God created us to walk in "precarious places"?

A Prayerful Response

Lord, I am willing to climb higher and higher with You. Amen.

THE ONLY SAFE PLACE

THOUGHT FOR TODAY

The cross is a safe dwelling place for believers.

WISDOM FROM SCRIPTURE

He [Jesus] called the crowd with his disciples, and said to them, "If any want to become my followers, let them deny themselves and take up their cross and follow me.

"For those who want to save their life will lose it, and those who lose their life for my sake, and for the sake of the gospel, will save it.

"For what will it profit them to gain the whole world and forfeit their life?

"Indeed, what can they give in return for their life?

"Those who are ashamed of me and of my words in this adulterous and sinful generation, of them the Son of Man will also be ashamed when he comes in the glory of his Father with the holy angels."

[Paul wrote:] Yet whatever gains I had, these I have come to regard as loss because of Christ.

More than that, I regard everything as loss because of the surpassing value of knowing Christ Jesus my Lord. For his sake I have suffered the loss of all things, and I regard them as rubbish, in order that I may gain Christ and be found in him, not having a righteousness of my own that comes from the law, but one that comes through faith in Christ, the righteousness from God based on faith.

I want to know Christ and the power of his resurrection and the sharing of his sufferings by becoming like him in his death, if somehow I may attain the resurrection from the dead.

Not that I have already obtained this or have already reached the goal; but I press on to make it my own, because Christ Jesus has made me his own.

Beloved, I do not consider that I have made it my own; but this one thing I do: forgetting what lies behind and straining forward to what lies ahead, I press on toward the goal for the prize of the heavenly call of God in Christ Jesus.

MARK 8:34-38; PHILIPPIANS 3:7-16, RSV

INSIGHTS FROM AMY CARMICHAEL

One morning I woke with these words on my lips: "We follow a stripped and crucified Savior."

Those words go very deep. They touch everything, one's outer life as well as one's inner: motives, purposes, decisions, everything. Let them be with you. You are sure to have tests as well as many an unexpected joy. But if you follow a stripped and crucified Savior, and by the power of His resurrection seek to enter into the fellowship of His sufferings, you will go on in peace and be one of those blessed ones who spread peace all around.

Deep in me, Lord, mark Thou Thy holy cross,
    On motives, choices, private dear desires;
Let all that self in any form inspires
    Be unto me as dross.

And when Thy touch of death is here and there
    Laid on a thing most precious in my eyes,
Let me wonder, let me recognize
    The answer to my prayer.

You are, by His grace, counted worthy to follow the crucified way of the cross. So few are ready for that. They preach about it, sing about it, but when it comes to *doing it*, then they just don't. But I should not say "they." "I" is the pronoun. What do I know of this way?

What [a friend] says is true, "The cross and the place of the fellowship of Christ's sufferings is the only safe place for those of us who have a responsibility for the souls of others." Never will you regret the fellowship of His sufferings.

I have been thinking today of our Lord's teaching in Mark 8:34 and kindred words. There is nothing offered on earth but a cross (and yet what joy is folded up in that offer!). He said unto all, "If any man would come after Me, let him deny himself, and take up his cross daily and follow Me" (Mark 8:34).

The Lord who did that Himself helps us to do so too, not in word and prayer only but in deed—common deed. Isn't it comforting, sometimes, to know that His eye sees a cross in something that doesn't look like anything of the sort to others?

And after all, is there anything in all the world to be compared with the joy of doing His will? I know of no joy like it.

—*Candles in the Dark*

Questions to Consider

1. In what ways do you take up your cross daily and follow Christ?

2. Why is the cross the "only safe place" for you?

A Prayerful Response

Lord, teach me to press on joyfully, following a stripped and crucified Savior. Amen.

GOLD BY MOONLIGHT

THOUGHT FOR TODAY

God plans good things for your future.

WISDOM FROM SCRIPTURE

For surely I know the plans I have for you, says the LORD, plans for your welfare and not for harm, to give you a future with hope.

Then when you call upon me and come and pray to me, I will hear you.

When you search for me, you will find me; if you seek me with all your heart, I will let you find me, says the LORD, and I will restore your fortunes and gather you from all the nations and all the places where I have driven you, says the LORD, and I will bring you back to the place from which I sent you into exile.

The human mind plans the way, but the LORD directs the steps.

All our steps are ordered by the LORD; how then can we understand our own ways? Our steps are made firm by the LORD, when he delights in our way; though we stumble, we shall not fall headlong, for the LORD holds us by the hand.

I know, O LORD, that the way of human beings is not in their control, that mortals as they walk cannot direct their steps.

Thus says the LORD, the God of Israel: Like these good figs, so I will regard as good the exiles from Judah, whom I have sent away from this place to the land of the Chaldeans.

I will set my eyes upon them for good, and I will bring them back to this land. I will build them up, and not tear them down; I will plant them, and not pluck them up.

I will give them a heart to know that I am the LORD; and they shall be my people and I will be their God, for they shall return to me with their whole heart.

JEREMIAH 29:11-14; PROVERBS 16:9; 20:24;
PSALMS 37:23-24; JEREMIAH 10:23; 24:5-7, RSV

INSIGHTS FROM AMY CARMICHAEL

"When heaven is about to confer a great office on a man it always first exercises his mind and soul with suffering, and his body with hunger, and exposes him to extreme poverty, and boggles all his undertakings. By these means it stimulates his mind, hardens his nature, and enables him to acts otherwise not possible to him," wrote Menicus, the Chinese sage, two thousand years ago.

The illustration of the Chladni plate beautifully shows how these agitating circumstances can be caused to work together for good. You sprinkle sand on a brass plate fixed on a pedestal, and draw a bow across the edge of the plate, touching it at the same time with two fingers. Then, because of this touch, the sand does not fall into confusion but into an ordered pattern like music made visible. Each little grain of sand finds its place in that pattern. Not one grain is forgotten and left to drift about unregarded.

There is nothing in the vibrations of the bow to make a pattern. Suffering, hunger, poverty, boggling circumstances cannot of themselves make anything but confusion. But if there be the touch of the Hand, all these things work together for good, not for all, not for discord, but for something like the harmony of music.

So the ruin is not out of sight, and thoughts wander round it at times. If it be loss, there is still an aching absence; if it be difficult circumstances, they will dominate the landscape; if it be limitations, they still confine us.

But what if the crash of hopes, the heartbreak, this that piles itself up as the ruin in the picture of life, does truly make more manifest what our Book calls the beauty of the Lord? If that be so, we should not wait till we are where life's poor ruins will appear as the tumbled bricks of a child's castle before we let our hearts take comfort from such words as these: *"I know the thoughts that I think toward you, saith the Lord, thoughts of peace and not of evil, to give you an expected end"* (Jeremiah 29:11).

Rotherham understands God's thoughts to mean His plans: "I know the plans which I am planning for you, plans of welfare and not of calamity, to give you a future and a hope." Thoughts of peace for our prayers, for our intercessions for others which seem to be ineffective. A future and a hope that we fear were covered by snow, and for those others that appeared to all on earth like the falling stars that break and scatter into nothingness as we watch them—even those prayers are folded up in the thoughts of peace that He thinks toward us.

These words are for us. We may take them though they were spoken to another people in another age. All the green fields of the Scriptures are for all the sheep of His pasture; none are fenced off from us. Our Lord and Savior, the great Shepherd of the sheep, Himself led the way into these fields, as a study of His use of the Old Testament shows. His servants, the writers of the New Testament, followed Him there; and so may we. The words of the Lord about His thoughts of peace are for us as well as for His ancient people Israel.

Hammer this truth out on the anvil of experience—this truth that the loving thoughts of God direct and perfect all that concerneth us. It will bear to be beaten out to the uttermost. The pledged word of God to man is no puffball to break at a touch and scatter into dust. It is iron. It is gold, the most malleable of all metals. It is more golden than gold. It abideth imperishable forever.

If we wait till we have clear enough vision to see the expected end before we stay our mind upon Him who is our strength, we shall miss an opportunity that will never come again. Now is the time to say, "My heart is fixed, O God, my heart is fixed: I will sing and give praise" (Psalms 57:7), even though as we say the words there is no sense of exultation.

I have been told, "It is possible to gather gold, where it may be had, with moonlight."

By moonlight, then, let us gather our gold.

—*Gold by Moonlight*

QUESTIONS TO CONSIDER

1. Why should you believe that God has good plans for you?

2. In what personal situation can you trust that God is working things together for good?

A PRAYERFUL RESPONSE

Lord, I believe Your plans for me are good, and I will wait for them. Amen.

Even the Death of the Cross

Thought for Today

You will find peace when you say, "Thy will be done."

Wisdom from Scripture

I will praise you, O LORD, with all my heart; before the "gods" I will sing your praise.

I will bow down toward your holy temple and will praise your name for your love and your faithfulness, for you have exalted above all things your name and your word.

When I called, you answered me; you made me bold and stouthearted.

May all the kings of the earth praise you, O LORD, when they hear the words of your mouth. May they sing of the ways of the LORD, for the glory of the LORD is great.

Though the LORD is on high, he looks upon the lowly, but the proud he knows from afar. Though I walk in the midst of trouble, you preserve my life; you stretch out your hand against the anger of my foes, with your right hand you save me.

The LORD will fulfill his purpose for me; your love, O LORD, endures forever—do not abandon the works of your hands. PSALM 138, NIV

You know the four Gospels tell the story of Gethsemane. Each is a little different, but all are true. They fit into one another and make a picture that, if you ever have to suffer, will mean everything to you.

I will take words from only two Gospels. In St. Mark we read that our Lord said, "Abba, Father, all things are possible unto Thee; *take away this cup from Me:* nevertheless not what I will, but what Thou wilt" (Mark 14:36). And in St. John we read that He said, *"The cup which My Father has given Me, shall I not drink it?"* (John 18:11).

You will have no peace until you pass from those first words to the second. But this may not come in a day. Be patient. He who prayed in agony that the cup might be removed will be patient with you, for He understands just what you are feeling. Yet He will not rest until He brings you to the place where He stood when He said, "The cup which My Father has given Me, shall I not drink it?"

I find much comfort in Psalms 138:3: "In the day when I cried Thou answeredest me and strengthenedest me with strength in my soul."

"In the day that I cried." That does not mean the day after, but *that very day, that very hour, that very minute.* God hears us the moment we cry and strengthens us with the only kind of strength that is of any use at all.

To each of us there is something that seems simply impossible to get on top of. I know my special foe and all this week I have had to live looking off to Jesus, the author and (thank God) the finisher of our faith. (I have just now turned to Hebrews 12:2 to make sure that word is really there.) Psalms 138:8 is another standby. Oh! blessed be the eternal Word of God. Feelings may change (they do), we may change and fall (we do), but His Word stands steadfast. It *cannot* fail.

Don't you think that some of us *must* know the trials of misty weather if we are to be enabled to understand when others are in the mist?

My word yesterday was *"Even* the death of the cross" (Philippians 2:8). There is an "even" in most lives. God help us not to shrink back from that "even."   —*Candles in the Dark*

QUESTIONS TO CONSIDER

1. What "even" is God calling you to embrace as His will?

2. How could the "misty weather" you endure help alleviate the suffering of others?

A PRAYERFUL RESPONSE

Lord, not my will, but Thy will be done in my life. Amen.

CAST NOT AWAY CONFIDENCE

THOUGHT FOR TODAY

Guard your confidence that God is in control.

WISDOM FROM SCRIPTURE

Therefore, my friends, since we have confidence to enter the sanctuary by the blood of Jesus, by the new and living way that he opened for us through the curtain (that is, through his flesh), and since we have a great priest over the house of God, let us approach with a true heart in full assurance of faith, with our hearts sprinkled clean from an evil conscience and our bodies washed with pure water.

Let us hold fast to the confession of our hope without wavering, for he who has promised is faithful.

And let us consider how to provoke one another to love and good deeds, not neglecting to meet together, as is the habit of some, but encouraging one another, and all the more as you see the Day approaching.

But recall those earlier days when, after you had been enlightened, you endured a hard struggle with sufferings, sometimes being publicly exposed to abuse and persecution, and sometimes being partners with those so treated.

For you had compassion for those who were in prison, and you cheerfully accepted the plundering of your possessions, knowing that you yourselves possessed something better and more lasting.

Do not, therefore, abandon that confidence of yours; it brings a great reward.

For you need endurance, so that when you have done the

will of God, you may receive what was promised.

For yet "in a very little while, the one who is coming will come and will not delay; but my righteous one will live by faith. My soul takes no pleasure in anyone who shrinks back."

But we are not among those who shrink back and so are lost, but among those who have faith and so are saved.

Now faith is the assurance of things hoped for, the conviction of things not seen.

Therefore… let us also lay aside every weight and the sin that clings so closely, and let us run with perseverance the race that is set before us, looking to Jesus the pioneer and perfecter of our faith, who for the sake of the joy that was set before him endured the cross, disregarding its shame, and has taken his seat at the right hand of the throne of God.

Consider him who endured such hostility against himself from sinners, so that you may not grow weary or lose heart.

HEBREWS 10:19-25, 32-39; 11:1, 39; 12:1-3, RSV

INSIGHTS FROM AMY CARMICHAEL

O my heart, welcome all that is sent to prepare and to brace thee for a generous tomorrow [in heaven]. Welcome barrenness, snow and frost, limitations, frustrations, the strain of uncertainty, steep ways, dull days. Welcome these things as the preparation for something made ready for thee before the foundations of the world.

Let thyself be broken. Let thyself be rent. Lay those keen yearnings in the hands that were wounded for thee. Let another gird thee and carry thee where thou will not go.

Let the winds blow, let the waves thunder; they cannot

uproot the rock. The wickedness of the wicked must come to an end, or God would not be God. If they do not consume away like a snail, so that we shall say, "Verily there is a reward for the righteous: doubtless there is a God that judgeth the earth" (Psalms 58:11), then there would be no God for us to worship.

But God Is. The coming of the Lord is as certain as the morning. The night will never return, with its brooding shadows of cruelty and wrong. Light, not darkness, is the ultimate conqueror. Not always shall our hearts cry out, *Lord, how long wilt Thou look upon this?* For sorrow and sighing shall flee away and the travail of the ages shall cease.

Cast not away, therefore, your confidence, which has great reward. He must reign. And He shall be as the light of the morning, when the sun rises, even a morning without clouds, and the glorious majesty of the Lord shall endure forever.

This assurance is among the things that cannot be shaken. So also is the peace that passeth all understanding, the peace of which He who is the Light and thy Salvation spoke long ago: *"Peace I leave with you, My peace I give unto you: not as the world giveth, give I unto you. Let not your heart be troubled, neither let it be afraid"* (John 14:27).   —*Figures of the True*

QUESTIONS TO CONSIDER

1. How can you welcome suffering?

2. How can you guard and grow your confidence in God?

A PRAYERFUL RESPONSE

Lord, even during suffering I will keep my confidence in You. Amen.

83

A Bruised Reed He Will Not Break

Thought for Today

God will not waste your pain.

Wisdom from Scripture

Here is my servant, whom I uphold, my chosen, in whom my soul delights; I have put my spirit upon him; he will bring forth justice to the nations.

He will not cry or lift up his voice, or make it heard in the street; a bruised reed he will not break, and a dimly burning wick he will not quench; he will faithfully bring forth justice.

He will not grow faint or be crushed until he has established justice in the earth; and the coastlands wait for his teaching.

Thus says God, the LORD, who created the heavens and stretched them out, who spread out the earth and what comes from it, who gives breath to the people upon it and spirit to those who walk in it:

I am the LORD, I have called you in righteousness, I have taken you by the hand and kept you; I have given you as a covenant to the people, a light to the nations, to open the eyes that are blind, to bring out the prisoners from the dungeon, from the prison those who sit in darkness.

I am the LORD, that is my name; my glory I give to no other, nor my praise to idols.

See, the former things have come to pass, and new things I now declare; before they spring forth, I tell you of them.

I will lead the blind by a road they do not know, by paths they have not known I will guide them. I will turn the darkness before them into light, the rough places into level ground. These are the things I will do, and I will not forsake them.

ISAIAH 42:1-9, 16, RSV

INSIGHTS FROM AMY CARMICHAEL

But to what end is pain? I do not clearly know. But I have noticed that when one who has not suffered draws near to one in pain there is rarely much power to help. There is not the understanding that leaves the suffering thing comforted, though perhaps not a word was spoken. I have wondered if it can be the same in the sphere of prayer.

Does pain accepted and endured give some quality that would otherwise be lacking in prayer? Does it create sympathy which can lay itself alongside the need, feeling it as though it were personal, so that it is possible to do just what the writer of Hebrews meant when he said, "Remember them that are in bonds, as bound with them, and them which suffer adversity, as being yourselves also in the body" (Hebrews 13:3)?

Most unforgettably we are also in the body. Often I wonder how any doctor, knowing what doctors do know, can have the heart to shut the door of the cage when the bird is ready to fly out. But that is foolishness, I suppose; after all, most birds want to stay in. However, the fact remains that the patients in the hospitals for incurables in every land, and in all other hospitals and places where the suffering be, are very conscious of the body. Apparently here is an opportunity.

What if every stroke of pain, or hour of weariness or loneliness, or any other trial of flesh or spirit, could carry us a pulsebeat nearer some other life, some life for which the ministry of prayer is needed; would it not be worthwhile to suffer? Ten thousand times yes. And surely it must be so, for the further we are drawn into the fellowship of Calvary with our dear Lord, the tenderer are we toward others, the closer alongside does our spirit lie with them that are in bonds; as being ourselves also in the body. God never wastes His children's pain.

"*A bruised reed shall He not break*" (Isaiah 42:4). The poorest shepherd boy on our South Indian hills is careful to choose, for the making of his flute, a reed that is straight and fine and quite unbruised. But our heavenly Shepherd often takes the broken and the bruised, and of such He makes His flutes.

But life, like His Book, is full of parables of tenderness; and one of these has often come into this room of late. For he whose name means "God's peace" has brought his autoharp to play to me, and has first tuned it while I expectantly waited for the music which I knew would follow the tuning.

Is music to come from our harp? Music of prayer, of praise, of consolation? The strings are relaxed, or perhaps too tensely stretched. Illness can cause either condition. But we have a Tuner.

Tune Thou my harp;
There is not, Lord, could never be,
The skill in me.

Tune Thou my harp;
That it may play Thy melody,
Thy harmony.

Tune Thou my harp;
O Spirit, breathe Thy thought through me,
As pleaseth Thee.   —*Rose From Brier*

QUESTIONS TO CONSIDER

1. How has God used your pain to help someone else?

2. How has God used someone else's suffering for good in your life?

A PRAYERFUL RESPONSE

Lord, help me to be tenderhearted to others as You have been to me. Amen.

DAY 21

Thou Hast Enlarged Me

Thought for Today

Pain can increase your intimacy with God.

Wisdom from Scripture

I consider that our present sufferings are not worth comparing with the glory that will be revealed in us.

The creation waits in eager expectation for the sons of God to be revealed. For the creation was subjected to frustration, not by its own choice, but by the will of the one who subjected it, in hope that the creation itself will be liberated from its bondage to decay and brought into the glorious freedom of the children of God.

We know that the whole creation has been groaning as in the pains of childbirth right up to the present time. Not only so, but we ourselves, who have the firstfruits of the Spirit, groan inwardly as we wait eagerly for our adoption as sons, the redemption of our bodies.

For in this hope we were saved. But hope that is seen is no hope at all. Who hopes for what he already has? But if we hope for what we do not yet have, we wait for it patiently.

In the same way, the Spirit helps us in our weakness. We do not know what we ought to pray for, but the Spirit himself intercedes for us with groans that words cannot express. And he who searches our hearts knows the mind of the Spirit, because the Spirit intercedes for the saints in accordance with God's will.

And we know that in all things God works for the good

of those who love him, who have been called according to his purpose.

For those God foreknew he also predestined to be conformed to the likeness of his Son, that he might be the firstborn among many brothers. And those he predestined, he also called; those he called, he also justified; those he justified, he also glorified.

What, then, shall we say in response to this? If God is for us, who can be against us? He who did not spare his own Son, but gave him up for us all—how will he not also, along with him, graciously give us all things?

Who will bring any charge against those whom God has chosen? It is God who justifies.

Who is he that condemns? Christ Jesus, who died—more than that, who was raised to life—is at the right hand of God and is also interceding for us.

Who shall separate us from the love of Christ? Shall trouble or hardship or persecution or famine or nakedness or danger or sword? As it is written: "For your sake we face death all day long; we are considered as sheep to be slaughtered."

No, in all these things we are more than conquerors through him who loved us. For I am convinced that neither death nor life, neither angels nor demons, neither the present nor the future, nor any powers, neither height nor depth, nor anything else in all creation, will be able to separate us from the love of God that is in Christ Jesus our Lord.

ROMANS 8:18-39, NIV

Thou hast enlarged me when I was in distress (Psalms 4:1).

The more one thinks of these words, the more they reveal their wonderful meaning. Darby renders it, "In pressure, Thou hast enlarged me," and Kay, "In straits Thou madest wide room for me." Whatever the pressure be, in that pressure— think of it—enlargement; the very opposite of what the word "pressure" suggests. And room, plenty of room, in a strait place.

We may sometimes feel distressed: here then is a word of pure hope and strong consolation. No distress need cramp us, crowd us into ourselves, make us smaller and poorer in anything that matters. Largeness, like the largeness of the sea, is His gift to us. We shall not be flattened in spirit by pressure, but enlarged. In the narrow ways of pain or of temptation He will make wide room for us.

During his long trial Job said, "Oh that I were as in months past, as in the days when God preserved me; when His candle shined upon my head, and when by His light I walked through darkness" (Job 29:2-3). Do we not all but see the heavenly watchers as they listened and longed that he might know what they had seen on those two days when Satan came among the sons of God and dared to challenge Him, and God took up the challenge (so brave is the love of God)? (See Job 1–2.)

But if Job had known, we should never have had that mighty story, nor would he ever have known his God as he knew Him at the end of that long tyranny. "I have heard of Thee by the hearing of the ear; but now mine eye seeth Thee" (42:5).

"And we know that the Son of God is come, and hath given us an understanding, that we may know Him that is true"

(1 John 5:20). This was my new light on Job. It cost Job what we know, and it cost John what we do not know (Patmos and all that lay behind and that followed after—the long martyrdom of life), to come to understand Him that is true.

In Job's deepest despondency he wished to be as he was when "the intimacy of God was over [his] tent" (Job 29:4, Rotherham), and he did not know that, even then, he was very near to a more wonderful intimacy than had ever been his before. Is it not joyful to think that it may be so with us?

Today, even today, we may be on the verge of—what?

—Thou Givest… They Gather

Questions to Consider

1. How can you allow God to enlarge you during distress?

2. This distress may place you on the verge of—what?

A Prayerful Response

Lord, please enlarge my relationship with You. Amen.

PART FOUR

THE PATH OF PERSEVERANCE

Long is the way, and very steep the slope,
Strengthen me once again, O God of Hope.

Far, very far, the summit doth appear;
But Thou art near my God, but Thou art near.

And Thou wilt give me with my daily food,
Powers of endurance, courage, fortitude.

Thy way is perfect; only let that way
Be clear before my feet from day to day.

Thou art my Portion, saith my soul to Thee,
O what a Portion is my God to me.

"THY WAY IS PERFECT," *TOWARD JERUSALEM*

AMY CARMICHAEL'S INSIGHT

There is great reward, both on earth and in heaven, for those who persevere in faith and obedience during trials.

DAY 22

HIS WAY IS PERFECT

THOUGHT FOR TODAY

When you can't see ahead, God still knows the way He's leading you.

WISDOM FROM SCRIPTURE

As the deer pants for streams of water, so my soul pants for you, O God. My soul thirsts for God, for the living God. When can I go and meet with God?

My tears have been my food day and night, while men say to me all day long, "Where is your God?"

These things I remember as I pour out my soul: how I used to go with the multitude, leading the procession to the house of God, with shouts of joy and thanksgiving among the festive throng.

Why are you downcast, O my soul? Why so disturbed within me? Put your hope in God, for I will yet praise him, my Savior and my God.

My soul is downcast within me; therefore I will remember you from the land of the Jordan, the heights of Hermon—from Mount Mizar. Deep calls to deep in the roar of your waterfalls; all your waves and breakers have swept over me.

By day the LORD directs his love, at night his song is with me—a prayer to the God of my life. I say to God my Rock, "Why have you forgotten me? Why must I go about mourning, oppressed by the enemy?"

My bones suffer mortal agony as my foes taunt me, saying to me all day long, "Where is your God?"

Why are you downcast, O my soul? Why so disturbed within me? Put your hope in God, for I will yet praise him, my Savior and my God.   PSALM 42, NIV

INSIGHTS FROM AMY CARMICHAEL

There was one who was not afraid of any evil tidings, for her heart stood fast believing in the Lord. And her trust was in the tender mercy of God forever and ever.

Often He had arisen as light in the darkness.

Often she had called upon Him in troubles and He had delivered her, and heard her when the storm fell upon her.

He had been merciful, loving and righteous, and she had said, "Who is like unto the Lord our God, that hath His dwelling so high; and yet humbleth Himself to behold the things that are in heaven and earth?" And now she found herself standing alone, looking into a great mist.

Fold after fold the hills lay there before her, but always in mist. She could see no path, except a little track in the valley below. She thought that she was quite alone, and for a while she stood looking, listening, and feeling this loneliness and uncertainty harder to bear than any acute distress had ever been.

Then, softly, voices began to speak with her, now discouraged, now encouraging.

"My flesh and my heart faileth. But God is the strength of my heart and my portion for ever" (Psalms 73:26).

"My lovers and my friends stand aloof from my soul; and my kinsmen stand afar off" (Psalms 38:11).

"Nevertheless, I am continually with Thee: Thou hast holden me by my right hand" (Psalms 73:23).

"My tears have been my meat day and night; while they continually say unto me, Where is thy God?" (Psalms 42:3).

"Thou shalt answer for me, O Lord my God" (Psalms 86:7).

"My way is hidden from my God" (Isaiah 40:27).

"He knoweth the way that I take. All my ways are before Him. As for God, His way is perfect and He maketh my way perfect. They thirsted not when He led them through the deserts. Will they faint when He leads them through the hills?" (Job 23:10; Psalms 119:68; 2 Samuel 22:31; Isaiah 48:21.)

Then she looked again at the mist, and it was lightening, and she knew that she was not alone, for her God was her refuge and strength, a very present help in trouble. He was about her path; He would make good His loving-kindness toward her, and His loving-kindness was comfortable. Nor could she fear anymore, for those dim folds in the hills were open ways to Him. He would not let her be disappointed in her hope.

So it was enough for her to see only the next few steps, because He would go before her and make His footsteps a way to walk in. And of this she was also sure: *He whom she followed saw through the mist to the end of the way.* She would never be put to confusion.

And in that hour a song was given to her. She sang it as she walked: "O what great troubles and adversities hast Thou showed me! and yet didst Thou turn and refresh me: and broughtest me up from the deep of the earth again. The Lord is my strength and my shield; my heart trusteth in Him, and I am helped; therefore my heart danceth for joy, and in my song will I praise Him" (Psalms 71:20; 28:7).

And as she walked thus and sang, others whom she did not see because of the mist that still lay on her way, heard her

singing and were comforted and helped to follow on, even
unto the end. —*Figures of the True*

QUESTIONS TO CONSIDER

1. What Scripture in today's reading comforts you the most?
2. Why can you place your hope in God, even when the way looks misty?

A PRAYERFUL RESPONSE

Lord, I don't know where we're headed, but I'm still trusting
and following You. Amen.

SWORDS DRAWN, UP TO THE GATES

THOUGHT FOR TODAY

God doesn't lay aside His soldiers.

WISDOM FROM SCRIPTURE

You then, my child, be strong in the grace that is in Christ Jesus; and what you have heard from me through many witnesses entrust to faithful people who will be able to teach others as well.

Share in suffering like a good soldier of Christ Jesus.

No one serving in the army gets entangled in everyday affairs; the soldier's aim is to please the enlisting officer. And in the case of an athlete, no one is crowned without competing according to the rules.

It is the farmer who does the work who ought to have the first share of the crops.

Think over what I say, for the Lord will give you understanding in all things.

Remember Jesus Christ, raised from the dead, a descendant of David—that is my gospel, for which I suffer hardship, even to the point of being chained like a criminal. But the word of God is not chained.

Therefore I endure everything for the sake of the elect, so that they may also obtain the salvation that is in Christ Jesus, with eternal glory.

The saying is sure: If we have died with him, we will also live with him; if we endure, we will also reign with him; if we deny him, he will also deny us; if we are faithless, he remains faithful—for he cannot deny himself.

Remind them of this, and warn them before God that they are to avoid wrangling over words, which does no good but only ruins those who are listening.

Do your best to present yourself to God as one approved by him, a worker who has no need to be ashamed, rightly explaining the word of truth.

Shun youthful passions and pursue righteousness, faith, love, and peace, along with those who call on the Lord from a pure heart. Have nothing to do with stupid and senseless controversies; you know that they breed quarrels.

And the Lord's servant must not be quarrelsome but kindly to everyone, an apt teacher, patient, correcting opponents with gentleness. God may perhaps grant that they will repent and come to know the truth, and that they may escape from the snare of the devil, having been held captive by him to do his will.   2 TIMOTHY 2:1-15, 22-26, RSV

INSIGHTS FROM AMY CARMICHAEL

Another of those words addressed to the sick came in a letter; it was about being "laid aside." It was the sort of thing one might say to a cracked china cup: "Poor dear, you are laid aside." But then the Lord's servant is not a china cup. He (she) is a soldier.

Soldiers may be wounded in battle and sent to a hospital. A hospital isn't a shelf; it is a place of repair. And a soldier on service in the spiritual army is never off his battlefield. He is only removed to another part of the field when a wound interrupts what he meant to do, and sets him doing something else.

So when a letter came from one who was about to join our

fellowship, quoting from his fiancée's letter to him, "I know that for us it is to be swords drawn, up to the gates of heaven," I found great delight in the word.

The song that came out of those words was written without a thought of my own minute and passing battle wound. I was thinking of the so much greater and more protracted trials that might be part of life for these two—for married life, if both husband and wife are pledged soldiers, is a sacrificial thing from the first day. And I would pass it on to all hurt soldiers everywhere. Is it not joy, pure joy, that there is no question of the shelf?

No soldier on service is ever "laid aside." He is only given another commission, sometimes just to suffer, sometimes, when pain and weakness lessen a little, to fight among the unseen forces of the field. Never, never is he shelved as of no further use to his beloved Captain. To feel so, even for a moment, is to be terribly weakened and disappointed; for, like these young recruits to our fellowship, did he not say from his first hour, "Swords drawn, up to the gates of heaven"?

And did not his Captain accept and enroll him, mere foot soldier in the ranks though he be, and is he not still following the colors? Blessed be the Lord of hosts, Captain and leader of all fighting men—it must be so, it *is* so: it can never be otherwise. Only, as I have been learning through these months, the soldier must let his captain say where, and for what, he needs him most, and he must not cloud his mind with questions. A wise master never wastes his servant's time, nor a commander his soldier's. There is great comfort in remembering that.

So let us settle it once for all and find heart's ease in doing so. There is no discharge in our warfare—no, not for a single day. We are never *hors de combat*. We may be called to serve on the visible field, going continually into the invisible both to renew our strength and to fight the kind of battle that can be fought only there. Or we may be called off the visible altogether for a while, and drawn into the invisible.

Those dread words "Laid aside" are never for us; we are soldiers of the King of kings. Soldiers are not shelved.

—*Rose From Brier*

QUESTIONS TO CONSIDER

1. Could the Lord be reassigning you to a new spiritual battlefield? How do you know?

2. What adjustments might accompany a new assignment?

A PRAYERFUL RESPONSE

Lord, thank You for not laying me aside in Your service. Amen.

RUN WITH PATIENCE

THOUGHT FOR TODAY

Heavenly endowed patience teaches us to endure.

WISDOM FROM SCRIPTURE

Consider it pure joy, my brothers, whenever you face trials of many kinds, because you know that the testing of your faith develops perseverance. Perseverance must finish its work so that you may be mature and complete, not lacking anything.

If any of you lacks wisdom, he should ask God, who gives generously to all without finding fault, and it will be given to him. But when he asks, he must believe and not doubt, because he who doubts is like a wave of the sea, blown and tossed by the wind. That man should not think he will receive anything from the Lord; he is a double-minded man, unstable in all he does.

The brother in humble circumstances ought to take pride in his high position. But the one who is rich should take pride in his low position, because he will pass away like a wild flower.

For the sun rises with scorching heat and withers the plant; its blossom falls and its beauty is destroyed. In the same way, the rich man will fade away even while he goes about his business.

Blessed is the man who perseveres under trial, because when he has stood the test, he will receive the crown of life that God has promised to those who love him.

When tempted, no one should say, "God is tempting

me." For God cannot be tempted by evil, nor does he tempt anyone; but each one is tempted when, by his own evil desire, he is dragged away and enticed. Then, after desire has conceived, it gives birth to sin; and sin, when it is full-grown, gives birth to death.

Don't be deceived, my dear brothers. Every good and perfect gift is from above, coming down from the Father of the heavenly lights, who does not change like shifting shadows.

He chose to give us birth through the word of truth, that we might be a kind of firstfruits of all he created.

JAMES 1:2-18, NIV

INSIGHTS FROM AMY CARMICHAEL

The unusualness, the unexpectedness, of the way thoughts and words are sometimes put together in the Bible set it apart from all other books. It is to me one of the innumerable touches that tell of the divine. No human writer would have written thus.

There is an example of this in Hebrews 12:1, *"Run with patience,"* which is like the word in Colossians 1:11, "Strengthened with all might, according to *His glorious power,* unto [not some flashing magnificence but just] *all patience."* The same verse holds another of these marks of the divine: *"longsuffering with joyfulness."* Which of us would have put these words together? But the Holy Spirit does.

Patience, Young says, means "endurance." Rotherham translates Hebrews 12:1, "With endurance let us be running," and so in Colossians 1:11, "With all power being empowered according to the grasp of His glory unto all endurance and longsuffering with joy."

I have been looking up the word in Young and find it comes much more frequently than the word which means only long-suffering. It is one of those trumpet-call words that sounds forth a challenge and stirs the heart and kindles it to rise and do.

As I thought of it this morning, I knew that life can offer us no greater gift than the opportunity to learn to endure. Should we wonder then that we have this gift sometimes? Should we wonder that the soul that follows hard after our Lord does invariably find itself in need of this special virtue? Should we wonder as though some strange thing happened unto us?

And as I thought of this I found something equally joyful and inspiring: Our God has chosen this very word to describe Himself, and with that word He links another, that dear word *consolation*, which means *encouragement*, the comfort that braces the soul. He is *the God of patience and consolation*, "the God of the endurance and of the encouragement." And this God is our God forever and ever.

"Many seem patient when they are not pricked." Richard Rolle said these words about six hundred years ago, and he quoted the old version of Proverbs 12:21: "Whatever happens to the righteous man *it shall not heavy him.*"

I have been thinking of four of the meanings of the word translated "endure" in our Authorized Version:

To remain under, as in Matthew 10:22; Hebrews 10:32; 12:2-3; and others.

To bear up under, 2 Timothy 3:11; 1 Peter 2:19.

To be long- or patient-minded, Hebrews 6:15.

To be strong, firm, Hebrews 11:27.

I wonder if these words can take to you what they brought

to me, but then I remember whose they are, and know that they will find the one for whom they are sent.

Are we finding it difficult to *remain under, bear up under,* something? Does it sometimes seem impossible to be truly, and for long, *patient-minded*? Do we feel far from being *strong, firm,* as our dear Lord was all through His holy life?

There is only one way of peace when we feel like that; it is to lay hold afresh on some sure word of promise or assurance. "My grace is sufficient for thee: for My strength is made perfect in weakness" (2 Corinthians 12:9). It is the word of Him who endured, to you and to me. It cannot fail. Our Lord said, "What things soever ye desire, when ye pray, believe that ye receive them, and ye shall have them" (Mark 11:24).

—*Thou Givest... They Gather*

Questions to Consider

1. What is the proof that someone "runs with patience"?
2. What can we expect if we follow hard after God?

A Prayerful Response

Lord, teach me the patience that endures. Amen.

DAY 25

LOOKING AT THINGS NOT SEEN

THOUGHT FOR TODAY

Faith grows when it focuses on "things not seen."

WISDOM FROM SCRIPTURE

But we have this treasure in jars of clay to show that this all-surpassing power is from God and not from us.

We are hard pressed on every side, but not crushed; perplexed, but not in despair; persecuted, but not abandoned; struck down, but not destroyed. We always carry around in our body the death of Jesus, so that the life of Jesus may also be revealed in our body.

For we who are alive are always being given over to death for Jesus' sake, so that his life may be revealed in our mortal body.

So then, death is at work in us, but life is at work in you. It is written: "I believed; therefore I have spoken." With that same spirit of faith we also believe and therefore speak, because we know that the one who raised the Lord Jesus from the dead will also raise us with Jesus and present us with you in his presence.

All this is for your benefit, so that the grace that is reaching more and more people may cause thanksgiving to overflow to the glory of God.

Therefore we do not lose heart. Though outwardly we are wasting away, yet inwardly we are being renewed day by day. For our light and momentary troubles are achieving for us an eternal glory that far outweighs them all.

So we fix our eyes not on what is seen, but on what is

unseen. For what is seen is temporary, but what is unseen is eternal.

Now we know that if the earthly tent we live in is destroyed, we have a building from God, an eternal house in heaven, not built by human hands.

Meanwhile we groan, longing to be clothed with our heavenly dwelling, because when we are clothed, we will not be found naked.

For while we are in this tent, we groan and are burdened, because we do not wish to be unclothed but to be clothed with our heavenly dwelling, so that what is mortal may be swallowed up by life.

Now it is God who has made us for this very purpose and has given us the Spirit as a deposit, guaranteeing what is to come. Therefore we are always confident and know that as long as we are at home in the body we are away from the Lord.

We live by faith, not by sight.

2 CORINTHIANS 4:7–5:7, NIV

INSIGHTS FROM AMY CARMICHAEL

"Not all... but at..." (2 Corinthians 4:18).

I have been finding help in laying the great story of 2 Kings 6:13-17 alongside the great words of 2 Corinthians 4:8-18. A host with horses and chariots was round about the city.... We are pressed on every side, perplexed, pursued, smitten down at times, always delivered unto death (see Revised Version).

"'Alas, my master! How shall we do?' And he answered, 'Fear not: for they that be with us are more than they that be with them.' And Elisha prayed, and said, 'Lord, I pray Thee, open his eyes, that he may see.' And the Lord opened the eyes of the young man; and he saw... [what had been there all the time] the mountain full of horses and chariots of fire round about Elisha" (2 Kings 6:15-17).

The secret of peace and courage is shown to us in this story, taken with the words that lead up to and follow after "While we look not at the things which are seen, but at the things which are not seen" (2 Corinthians 4:18). So let us live, not in the visible but in the invisible, not in the temporal but in the eternal.

While our eyes are fixed on our trouble—"the things which are seen"—those troubles are doing nothing for us; they are useless. But while our eyes are fixed, not on our troubles but on something beyond—"the things which are not seen"— those troubles have a wonderful power to work for us.

We are not told how it is they have this power, or how they use their power, only that they have it: "For our light affliction, which is but for a moment, worketh for us a far more exceeding and eternal weight of glory; while we look not at the things which are seen, but at the things which are not seen: for the things which are seen are temporal; but the things which are not seen are eternal" (verses 17-18).

I have often thanked God for telling us this heavenly secret. It helps so very much in hard times. Job, and Joseph, and Moses, and Paul, and many others in Bible times, and countless numbers since then, came through hard days when rushing blows fell upon them, like wave upon wave beating on their souls. But they know now what the exceeding and eternal weight of glory is. Are they sorry now, as they look back, that they endured? I think not.

We can only go in peace as we see "Him who is invisible,"

that is, as we look always from the trial to the Lord. This is what Moses did, and so he was able to endure. "Where there is no vision, the people perish" (Proverbs 29:18).

If we see only the things of time, and forget the things of eternity, we perish, our faith withers and we become weak and hopeless. We need vision for life, vision for prayer, continual undimmed vision, if we are to be those on whom our God can count for anything, any time, anywhere.

—*Thou Givest… They Gather*

QUESTIONS TO CONSIDER

1. On what "unseen things" do you need to focus?

2. What could keep you from focusing on the unseen?

A PRAYERFUL RESPONSE

Lord, sharpen my vision to focus on the unseen. Amen.

THE SECRET OF ENDURANCE

THOUGHT FOR TODAY

The secret of endurance resides in God's character.

WISDOM FROM SCRIPTURE

To you I call, O LORD my Rock; do not turn a deaf ear to me. For if you remain silent, I will be like those who have gone down to the pit.

Hear my cry for mercy as I call to you for help, as I lift up my hands toward your Most Holy Place.

Do not drag me away with the wicked, with those who do evil, who speak cordially with their neighbors but harbor malice in their hearts. Repay them for their deeds and for their evil work; repay them for what their hands have done and bring back upon them what they deserve. Since they show no regard for the works of the LORD and what his hands have done, he will tear them down and never build them up again.

Praise be to the LORD, for he has heard my cry for mercy. The LORD is my strength and my shield; my heart trusts in him, and I am helped. My heart leaps for joy and I will give thanks to him in song. The LORD is the strength of his people, a fortress of salvation for his anointed one.

Save your people and bless your inheritance; be their shepherd and carry them forever.   PSALM 28, NIV

Insights from Amy Carmichael

Note: Amy wrote these excerpts as conversations between the heavenly Father and one of His earthbound sons.

The son asked for the grace of continuance. His Father showed him a waterfall fed from unseen fountains. The river of God is full of water, was His word then.

The son feared the chilly influences of life. His Father showed him an altar. All night the fire burned there. The fire shall ever be burning upon the altar; it shall never go out.

Then the son remembered that as the fall was fed to water from above, so the fire of the altar was lighted by fire that came from before the Lord.

The son asked, What is the secret of continued endurance?

His Father answered, It is found in seeing Him who is invisible. It is found in looking at the joy that is set before thee. It is found in considering Him who endured. It is found in taking for thine own the words of one who was tempted to wax faint, "In the day when I cried Thou answered me, and strengthened me with strength in my soul" (Psalms 138:3).

It is found in staking thine all upon the highest word of the Lord, thy Redeemer. It is found in loyalty. It is found in love.

—*His Thoughts Said… His Father Said*

Questions to Consider

1. In what ways is God's character enduring?

2. How can you exhibit this same endurance?

A Prayerful Response

Lord, I will look to You for endurance. Amen.

IS THINE HEART SET ON ASCENTS?

THOUGHT FOR TODAY

God can keep your heart set on spiritual ascents.

WISDOM FROM SCRIPTURE

LORD, who may dwell in your sanctuary? Who may live on your holy hill?

He whose walk is blameless and who does what is righteous, who speaks the truth from his heart and has no slander on his tongue, who does his neighbor no wrong and casts no slur on his fellowman, who despises a vile man but honors those who fear the LORD, who keeps his oath even when it hurts, who lends his money without usury and does not accept a bribe against the innocent. He who does these things will never be shaken.

Keep me safe, O God, for in you I take refuge. I said to the LORD, "You are my LORD; apart from you I have no good thing."

As for the saints who are in the land, they are the glorious ones in whom is all my delight. The sorrows of those will increase who run after other gods. I will not pour out their libations of blood or take up their names on my lips.

LORD, you have assigned me my portion and my cup; you have made my lot secure. The boundary lines have fallen for me in pleasant places; surely I have a delightful inheritance.

I will praise the LORD, who counsels me; even at night my heart instructs me. I have set the LORD always before me. Because he is at my right hand, I will not be shaken.

Therefore my heart is glad and my tongue rejoices; my

body also will rest secure, because you will not abandon me to the grave, nor will you let your Holy One see decay.

You have made known to me the path of life; you will fill me with joy in your presence, with eternal pleasures at your right hand.   PSALMS 15–16, NIV

INSIGHTS FROM AMY CARMICHAEL

Note: Today's readings are more conversations between the Father and son.

His thoughts said, The coil of circumstances is beyond anything I ever experienced before.

His Father said, All this assemblage of complicated circumstances is the massif [backbone] of the mountains thou must climb. There is a way among the boulders of the moraine [masses of rocks], between the seracs [pinnacles of ice] of the glaciers, over the snow-bridges that cross the crevasses [cracks], round the overhanging snow-fields and up the precipices and long aretes [narrow ridges].

There is a way through the deep shadows that will seem to bar thy path at times. Press on, press on to the summit.

His thoughts said, The rocks are far too steep for me. I cannot climb.

His Father said, With Me as thy guide, thou canst. I have not given thee the spirit of fear, but of power and of love and of discipline (2 Timothy 1:7). Why then this spirit of fear?

His thoughts said, But who shall ascend unto the hill of the Lord or who shall rise up in His holy place (Psalms 24:3)? Shall I ever pass the foothills?

His Father said, Is thine heart set on ascents?

The son answered, O Lord, Thou knowest.

And the Father comforted him, Commit thy way—thy way to the summit—to thy Lord. Only let thine heart be set on ascents.

And the Father added, Dear son, I will keep thine heart set on ascents.

After a time of tension his thoughts said, It is written of David, David was dispirited. I am dispirited. I cannot speak to anyone of the cause. It is private.

His Father said, I heard thee in the secret place of the storm. In the secret place among the unspoken things, there am I.

The son answered, When I am poor and in heaviness, Thy help, O Lord, doth lift me up.

And His Father said, Cast not away therefore thy confidence which has great reward (Hebrews 10:35).

—His Thoughts Said... His Father Said

Questions to Consider

1. What "ascent" do you want to reach?

2. How can you be sure this is a God-given ascent?

A Prayerful Response

Lord, keep my heart set on godly ascents. Amen.

TAKE THE NEXT STEP

THOUGHT FOR TODAY

God leads you one step at a time.

WISDOM FROM SCRIPTURE

Your word is a lamp to my feet and a light to my path. Therefore let all who are faithful offer prayer to you; at a time of distress, the rush of mighty waters shall not reach them.

You are a hiding place for me; you preserve me from trouble; you surround me with glad cries of deliverance.

I will instruct you and teach you the way you should go; I will counsel you with my eye upon you. Do not be like a horse or a mule, without understanding, whose temper must be curbed with bit and bridle, else it will not stay near you.

Many are the torments of the wicked, but steadfast love surrounds those who trust in the LORD.

The LORD will guide you continually, and satisfy your needs in parched places, and make your bones strong; and you shall be like a watered garden, like a spring of water, whose waters never fail.

Your ancient ruins shall be rebuilt; you shall raise up the foundations of many generations; you shall be called the repairer of the breach, the restorer of streets to live in.

If you refrain from trampling the sabbath, from pursuing your own interests on my holy day; if you call the sabbath a delight and the holy day of the LORD honorable; if you honor it, not going your own ways, serving your own interests, or pursuing your own affairs; then you shall take delight in the LORD, and I will make you ride upon the heights of the earth; I will feed you with the heritage of your ancestor Jacob, for the mouth of the LORD has spoken.

PSALMS 119:105; 32:6-10; ISAIAH 58:11-14, RSV

INSIGHTS FROM AMY CARMICHAEL

I think that in guidance God deals with us as He dealt with the Israelites. The first crossing of the seas was made very easy, the guidance could not have been simpler. The strong east wind blew and divided the sea before the people had to cross; not a foot was wet, except perhaps by the driving spray.

But how different it was on the second occasion, when God taught them to obey without, as it were, making it first of all impossible to disobey. The priests had to stand still in the water of the river. What a gift for men to scoff at, that standing still in the water! But it was not till they obeyed, and without a particle of visible proof that they were doing right, went on to carry the ark right into the river, that the water rolled back before them.

So, it seems to me, as we go on with God we may be called again and again to go right into our rivers, to wet our feet in them. We may be called to do what nobody understands except those to whom the word and the promise has come. But the word must come first and the promise too. We must be sure, with an inward conviction that absolutely nothing can shake.

In my own case I have had to wet my feet in the water again and again. But when the Red Sea kind of guidance is given I am always very glad, for then others can see, and that does help. You know those lines in Hannington's *Life:*

> He saw a hand they could not see
> That beckoned him away,
> He heard a voice they could not hear
> That would not let him stay.

Only God and those who have to walk in that path know how hard it can be. But He does know, and when the people about us don't hear the words of the voice, but only say, "It thunders," well, He comes near, and we know Him as we never knew Him before. At least it seems so to me.

I think the picture of the unwetted feet in the first crossing over water, and the wetted feet in the second, when a lesson of guidance far deeper than the first had to be given, is full of teaching for us. What I would think much more of is that inward urge; and as for outward things, well, no need to speak of them. To the watching eye and the listening ear they are clear enough. And then with that usually comes a loving word of peace.

But for the present there is just the thing to be done. Never let a possible tomorrow muddle up today, or shadow it, or confuse it. Nothing that comes in the day's work is waste; it will all fit in one day.

If the next step is clear, then the one thing to do is to take it. Don't pledge your Lord or yourself about the steps beyond. You don't see them yet.

Once when I was climbing at night in the forest before there was a made path, I learned what the word meant in Psalms 119:105: "Thy word is a *lantern* to my path." I had a lantern and had to hold it very low or I should certainly have slipped on those rough rocks.

We don't walk spiritually by electric light but by a hand lantern. And a lantern only shows the next step—not several ahead. —*Candles in the Dark*

Questions to Consider

1. In what way might God be calling you to "wet your feet"?
2. What "next step" is He waiting for you to take?

A Prayerful Response

Lord, I will take the next step You ask of me. Amen.

DAY 29

THE LORD'S DIEHARDS

THOUGHT FOR TODAY

It is an honor for God to trust you with difficulty.

WISDOM FROM SCRIPTURE

Be patient, therefore, beloved, until the coming of the Lord. The farmer waits for the precious crop from the earth, being patient with it until it receives the early and the late rains.

You also must be patient. Strengthen your hearts, for the coming of the Lord is near.

Beloved, do not grumble against one another, so that you may not be judged. See, the Judge is standing at the doors!

As an example of suffering and patience, beloved, take the prophets who spoke in the name of the Lord.

Indeed we call blessed those who showed endurance. You have heard of the endurance of Job, and you have seen the purpose of the Lord, how the Lord is compassionate and merciful.

Above all, my beloved, do not swear, either by heaven or by earth or by any other oath, but let your "Yes" be yes and your "No" be no, so that you may not fall under condemnation.

Are any among you suffering? They should pray. Are any cheerful? They should sing songs of praise.

Are any among you sick? They should call for the elders of the church and have them pray over them, anointing them with oil in the name of the Lord. The prayer of faith will save the sick, and the Lord will raise them up; and anyone who has committed sins will be forgiven.

Therefore confess your sins to one another, and pray for one another, so that you may be healed. The prayer of the righteous is powerful and effective.

Elijah was a human being like us, and he prayed fervently that it might not rain, and for three years and six months it did not rain on the earth.

For this very reason, you must make every effort to support your faith with goodness, and goodness with knowledge, and knowledge with self-control, and self-control with endurance, and endurance with godliness, and godliness with mutual affection, and mutual affection with love.

For if these things are yours and are increasing among you, they keep you from being ineffective and unfruitful in the knowledge of our Lord Jesus Christ.

For anyone who lacks these things is nearsighted and blind, and is forgetful of the cleansing of past sins. Therefore, brothers and sisters, be all the more eager to confirm your call and election, for if you do this, you will never stumble. JAMES 5:7-17; 2 PETER 1:5-11, RSV

Insights from Amy Carmichael

"Die hard, my men, die hard!" shouted Colonel Inglis of the 57th to his men on the heights behind the river Albuhera. The regiment was nicknamed the Diehards after that. The tale may have been forgotten but the name lives on, and in spite of foolish uses it is a great name. It challenges us.

We are called to be the Lord's diehards to whom can be committed any kind of trial of endurance, and who can be counted upon to stand firm whatever happens. It is written of Cromwell: "He strove to give his command so strict a unity that in no crisis should it crack." With this aim in view he made his Ironsides. The result of that discipline was seen not only in victory but in defeat; for his troops, "though they were beaten and routed, presently rallied again and stood in good order till they received new orders" (*Oliver Cromwell* by John Buchan).

This is the spirit that animates all valiant life: to be strong in will—to strive, to seek, to find, and not to yield—is all that ever matters. Failure or success, as the world understands these words, is of no eternal account. To be able to stand steady in defeat is in itself a victory. There is no tinsel about that kind of triumph.

Wind means stress and strain. "The elastic limit" of each kind of tree is known to the engineer, and he deals accordingly with his timber. So does the creator of the trees, the commander of the winds, know the "elastic limit" of His trees. And he knows the weight of the winds. "He looketh to the ends of the earth, to make the weight for the winds" (Job 28:24-25).

The weight of the winds can be tremendous. Here is one who has great gifts of mind but who, because of some structural trouble in the head, cannot read or listen to reading. To be free from severe and persistent pain only when utterly quiescent, and yet to be kept in peace, is surely something very greatly to the glory of His grace. Here is another, shattered, paralyzed and blinded. That wind can tear the branches from the pine.

"Nothing but the finite pity is sufficient for the infinite pathos of life," but that is only half a truth. *Nothing but the courageous love of God is brave enough to trust the soul of man to endure as seeing Him who is invisible; and nothing but the grace of God.*

There is a curious comfort in remembering that the Father depends upon His child to not give way. It is inspiring to be trusted with a hard thing.   —*Gold by Moonlight*

Questions to Consider

1. What is honorable about the difficulty God has entrusted to you?

2. How can you inspire others to be "diehards" in spiritual battle?

A Prayerful Response

Lord, thank You for honoring me with a difficult task. Amen.

THE NEVER-ENDING SUPPLY

THOUGHT FOR TODAY

When you lack what you need, God can supply it.

WISDOM FROM SCRIPTURE

I will extol you, O LORD, for you have drawn me up, and did not let my foes rejoice over me.

O LORD my God, I cried to you for help, and you have healed me.

O LORD, you brought up my soul from Sheol, restored me to life from among those gone down to the Pit.

Sing praises to the LORD, O you his faithful ones, and give thanks to his holy name.

For his anger is but for a moment; his favor is for a lifetime. Weeping may linger for the night, but joy comes with the morning.

As for me, I said in my prosperity, "I shall never be moved."

By your favor, O LORD, you had established me as a strong mountain; you hid your face; I was dismayed.

To you, O LORD, I cried, and to the LORD I made supplication: "What profit is there in my death, if I go down to the Pit? Will the dust praise you? Will it tell of your faithfulness?

"Hear, O LORD, and be gracious to me! O LORD, be my helper!"

You have turned my mourning into dancing; you have taken off my sackcloth and clothed me with joy, so that my soul may praise you and not be silent. O LORD my God, I will give thanks to you forever.

Do not fret because of the wicked; do not be envious of wrongdoers, for they will soon fade like the grass, and wither like the green herb.

Trust in the LORD, and do good; so you will live in the land, and enjoy security.

Take delight in the LORD, and he will give you the desires of your heart.

Commit your way to the LORD; trust in him, and he will act.

He will make your vindication shine like the light, and the justice of your cause like the noonday.

Be still before the LORD, and wait patiently for him; do not fret over those who prosper in their way, over those who carry out evil devices. PSALMS 30; 37:1-7, RSV

INSIGHTS FROM AMY CARMICHAEL

There was a time in the story of Dohnavur when the work that meant far more than life to us all was tossed about and beaten up like the little ship on the Sea of Galilee. It seemed impossible that it should survive, it was so helpless, so defenseless in the eyes of men.

One day it was a very turbulent day, the thought of that ship in the teeth of the gale was like light breaking through the rack that was tearing across the sky, and our hearts kept on saying over and over, "What matter beating wind and tossing billow if only we are in the boat with Thee?" till at last the word was spoken, "Peace, be still" (Mark 4:39), and there was great calm.

And so, as one who has known the blowing of the winds I say to the fearful, "Fear not, There is nothing to fear, nor ever can be, if our Lord be in the boat. O taste and see that the Lord is good: blessed is the man that trusteth in Him. There is nothing too kind for Him to do for the man that trusteth in Him" (Psalms 34:8).

The trial of the hour may be of the body, of the mind and spirit, or of circumstances; whatever it be, the same love can comfort. "If your Lord calls you to suffering, be not dismayed; there shall be a new allowance of the King for you when you come to it."

We are not at the mercy of wind and wave. We live a double life. Forces of distress may assail us (as they continually assailed our Lord), and we are called to labor from the rising of the morning till the stars appear, and yet all the time in the inner life of the spirit we are marvelously renewed, and raised up and made to sit together in heavenly places in Christ Jesus.

It is the Blessed One and no other who stands by us on the hill when the storm descends upon us. (O Christ, hadst Thou not suffered, how couldst Thou help us now?) And He who suffered and who overcame will grant us also to overcome. I can think of no truer picture of what we want to be when the wind beats on us for the last time, than this pine, broken and battered, but not uprooted, standing steadfast, undefeated—*and not alone.*

And now, O my soul, settle it with thyself that thou wilt listen to no hard reports which the ills of this present time may make to thee concerning thy Lord, for "nothing can come wrong for my Lord in His sweet working." Not clouds and dark woods, for they are lighted; not the deep ravine, for it leads to the heights; not snow, for it can cherish; not ruin, for "He can make one web of contraries"; not rough waters, for they cannot overfloweth; not steep mountains, for when I said, "My foot slippeth," Thy mercy, O Lord, held me up (Psalms 94:18); not dark woods again, for I do not build my nest in any tree on earth; not walls, for they have windows; not storms, for they cannot uproot me; not loneliness, for I am not alone.

"Only be thou strong and very courageous." This is Thy word to me, O Lord. "As I was with Moses so I will be with thee: I will not fail thee nor forsake thee. Be strong and of good courage" (Joshua 1:5-7). Courage that dares, fortitude that endures—without these I am a reed shaken with the wind. Surely fortitude is the sovereign virtue of life; not patience, though we need it too, but fortitude. O God, give me fortitude. *—Gold by Moonlight*

Questions to Consider
1. What do you need supplied to you today?
2. Why can you trust that God will come through for you?

A Prayerful Response
Lord, thank You for Your never-ending supply. Amen.

PART FIVE

A REASON FOR JOY

Are these the days when thou dost gird thyself
And walkest where thou wouldest, battle days,
Crowded and burdened and yet lit with praise,
Days of adventure; eager, glorious choice
Folded in every hour? Rejoice, rejoice,
O happy warrior, if so it be,
 For surely thou shalt see
Jesus Himself draw near and walk with thee.

Or doth another gird thee, carry thee
Whither thou wouldest not, and doth a cord
Bind hand and foot, and flying thought and word?
An enemy hath done it, even so,
(Though why that power was his thou dost not know).
O happy captive, fettered and yet free,
Believe, believe to see
Jesus Himself draw near and walk with thee.

So either way is blessed; either way
Leadeth unto the Lord of Heart's Desire;
Thy great Companion's love can never tire;
He is thy Confidence, He is thy Song;
Let not thy heart be troubled, but be strong,
O happy soul, to whom is given to see
On all the roads that be,
Jesus Himself draw near and walk with thee.

"ANOTHER SHALL GIRD THEE," *TOWARD JERUSALEM*

129

Amy Carmichael's Insight

Even during the worst of times, if you submit to Him you can live with God's joy and songs in your soul.

THE LIFTING POWER OF PRAISE

THOUGHT FOR TODAY

Praising God can lift a downcast spirit.

WISDOM FROM SCRIPTURE

Great is the LORD, and most worthy of praise, in the city of our God, his holy mountain. It is beautiful in its loftiness, the joy of the whole earth. Like the utmost heights of Zaphon is Mount Zion, the city of the Great King. God is in her citadels; he has shown himself to be her fortress.

When the kings joined forces, when they advanced together, they saw her and were astounded; they fled in terror. Trembling seized them there, pain like that of a woman in labor. You destroyed them like ships of Tarshish shattered by an east wind.

As we have heard, so have we seen in the city of the LORD Almighty, in the city of our God: God makes her secure forever.

Within your temple, O God, we meditate on your unfailing love. Like your name, O God, your praise reaches to the ends of the earth; your right hand is filled with righteousness.

Mount Zion rejoices, the villages of Judah are glad because of your judgments. Walk about Zion, go around her, count her towers, consider well her ramparts, view her citadels, that you may tell of them to the next generation.

For this God is our God for ever and ever; he will be our guide even to the end.   PSALM 48, NIV

Insights from Amy Carmichael

"I would rejoice in the mountains to climb, but I see no mountains. I see only a dreary waste of water, a drearier strip of shore; nothing invigorating, nothing inspiring, nothing hard enough to inspire.

"My life is just like that—not so much hard as dull, and I would have chosen the hard to the last; not mere negation, but achievement at whatever cost. It is the inability to do that is so devastating."

"Hast thou looked up?"

"Up? I see a mass of clouds. That is all."

"And nothing beyond the clouds? O look again. Is there no hint of light beyond? Are not the very clouds a marvel of controlled power, pillars of cloud and of fire?"

"My sight faileth me for waiting so long upon my God."

"So long? Ye have need of patience, that, after ye have done the will of God, ye might receive the promise" (Hebrews 10:36).

"It is written, 'As for me, when I am poor and in heaviness: Thy help, O God, shall lift me up.' I waited to be lifted up."

"But it is also written, 'As for me, I will patiently abide always: and will praise Thee more and more.' *Hast thou tried the lifting power of praise?"*

"My sight faileth because of trouble. How can I praise when I cannot see?"

"We can sing when we cannot see; even a little bird will sing in the grey dusk before the dawn breaks."

"My soul melteth away for every heaviness. Who can sing when his soul melteth?"

"Tell me, is not thy heart's desire to bring many people into glory?"

"That is all I desire."

"Then there is only one way for thee; I know of no other way. If thou would be inwardly victorious and help others to be victors, thou must refuse to be dominated by the seen and the felt. *Thou must look steadfastly through the visible till the invisible opens to thee.*

"This is harder than to climb a mountain. It is indeed to climb out of the lowest abyss where the craven soul can crawl, and to walk on the sunlit uplands. It is to live in the spirit of the words of one who was to look out upon a duller stretch of water and a darker strip of shore than thou dost now. Ponder then his words: *'For our light affliction, which is but for a moment, worketh for us a far more exceeding and eternal weight of glory; while we look not at the things which are seen, but at the things which are not seen: for the things which are seen are temporal; but the things which are not seen are eternal'* (2 Corinthians 4:17-18).

"Live by the grace of thy Lord in the spirit of these words for in them is the quality of eternity. Say of the will of thy God, 'I am content to do it.' Go through that depressing dimness without yielding to depression and without depressing others. All the resources of heaven are at thy command to enable thee to do this. Take a single promise of thy God; lean thy full weight upon it, and soon, very soon, thou wilt sing of the Lord because He hath dealt so lovingly with thee."

—*Figures of the True*

Questions to Consider

1. What are the "clouds" in your life that keep you from rejoicing?

2. For what can you praise God?

A Prayerful Response

Lord, I praise You for Your presence and power in my life. Amen.

As Glad and Merry As Possible

Thought for Today

Focusing on Jesus can evoke joy.

Wisdom from Scripture

Happy are those whose way is blameless, who walk in the law of the LORD.

Happy are those who keep his decrees, who seek him with their whole heart, who also do no wrong, but walk in his ways.

You have commanded your precepts to be kept diligently. O that my ways may be steadfast in keeping your statutes! Then I shall not be put to shame, having my eyes fixed on all your commandments.

I will praise you with an upright heart, when I learn your righteous ordinances. I will observe your statutes; do not utterly forsake me.

How can young people keep their way pure? By guarding it according to your word.

With my whole heart I seek you; do not let me stray from your commandments.

I treasure your word in my heart, so that I may not sin against you.

Blessed are you, O LORD; teach me your statutes. With my lips I declare all the ordinances of your mouth.

I delight in the way of your decrees as much as in all riches. I will meditate on your precepts, and fix my eyes on your ways. I will delight in your statutes; I will not forget your word.

Deal bountifully with your servant, so that I may live and observe your word. Open my eyes, so that I may behold wondrous things out of your law.

I live as an alien in the land; do not hide your commandments from me. My soul is consumed with longing for your ordinances at all times.

You rebuke the insolent, accursed ones, who wander from your commandments; take away from me their scorn and contempt, for I have kept your decrees.

Even though princes sit plotting against me, your servant will meditate on your statutes. Your decrees are my delight, they are my counselors. My soul clings to the dust; revive me according to your word.

When I told of my ways, you answered me; teach me your statutes.

Make me understand the way of your precepts, and I will meditate on your wondrous works.

My soul melts away for sorrow; strengthen me according to your word.

Put false ways far from me; and graciously teach me your law.

I have chosen the way of faithfulness; I set your ordinances before me. I cling to your decrees, O LORD; let me not be put to shame. I run the way of your commandments, for you enlarge my understanding.

Teach me, O LORD, the way of your statutes, and I will observe it to the end. PSALMS 119:1-33, RSV

Nearly five hundred years ago Julian of Norwich wrote when she was earnestly thinking of our Lord's suffering, and trying to see His dying,

> Suddenly, He changed the look of His blessed countenance. The changing of His blessed countenance changed mine, and I was as glad and merry as it was possible. Then brought our Lord merrily to my mind: "Where is now any point of the pain or of thy grief?" And I was full merry.

But this is only the beginning. The heart cannot conceive the joy that is drawing nearer every day—the joy that shall be ours when we are where there will be no more withering or fear of withering.

So she was "full merry." If it can be this now, what will be when we shall see Him, and we shall speak face to face?

It seems to me clear beyond question that in the lives of God's beloved there are sometimes periods when the adversary is "given power to overcome." The power need never overwhelm the inner courts of the spirit, but it may press hard on the outworks of being.

And so I have been asking that our dearest Lord may have the joy (surely it must be a joy to Him) of saying about each one of us, and about us all as a little company of His children: "I can count on him, or her, or them for *anything*. I can count on them for peace under any disappointment or series of disappointments, under any strain. I can trust them never to set limits, saying 'Thus far, and no farther.' I can trust them not to offer the reluctant obedience of a doubtful faith, but to be as glad and merry as it is possible."   —*Rose From Brier*

QUESTIONS TO CONSIDER

1. In what areas of your walk with God are you setting limits or following Him with a "reluctant obedience"?

2. How can you learn to find joy in Jesus?

A PRAYERFUL RESPONSE

Lord, I long to find joy in You. Amen.

THY WILL BE MY WILL

THOUGHT FOR TODAY

God's will can delight and bring peace to your heart.

WISDOM FROM SCRIPTURE

"Do not let your hearts be troubled. Believe in God, believe also in me.

"In my Father's house there are many dwelling places. If it were not so, would I have told you that I go to prepare a place for you? And if I go and prepare a place for you, I will come again and will take you to myself, so that where I am, there you may be also. And you know the way to the place where I am going."

Thomas said to him, "Lord, we do not know where you are going. How can we know the way?"

Jesus said to him, "I am the way, and the truth, and the life. No one comes to the Father except through me. If you know me, you will know my Father also. From now on you do know him and have seen him.

"Very truly, I tell you, the one who believes in me will also do the works that I do and, in fact, will do greater works than these, because I am going to the Father.

"I will do whatever you ask in my name, so that the Father may be glorified in the Son. If in my name you ask me for anything, I will do it.

"Those who love me will keep my word, and my Father will love them, and we will come to them and make our home with them.

"Whoever does not love me does not keep my words;

and the word that you hear is not mine, but is from the Father who sent me.

"I have said these things to you while I am still with you.

"But the Advocate, the Holy Spirit, whom the Father will send in my name, will teach you everything, and remind you of all that I have said to you.

"Peace I leave with you; my peace I give to you. I do not give to you as the world gives. Do not let your hearts be troubled, and do not let them be afraid."

JOHN 14:1-7, 12-14, 23-27, RSV

INSIGHTS FROM AMY CARMICHAEL

"But sometimes it cometh to our mind that we have prayed a long time, and yet we think to ourselves that we have not what we ask. But we should not be in heaviness. For I am sure, by our Lord's signifying, that either we abide a better time, or more grace, or a better gift."

So said Julian of Norwich. One of the better gifts is the sweetness of our daily manna, which when we can only gather a very little, a mere handful, is somehow caused to suffice so that we have no lack. A single thought of love opens out, like a bud opening into flower before our eyes, as, indeed, the large violet passionflower of South India does, between nine and ten every morning, whether growing or in a bowl by one's bedside—and a wonderful thing it is to see.

Another of the better gifts is the power which is all divine, not in the least of us, to acquiesce with true inward peace in that which our Lord allows to be, so that it is not an effort to be happy, we *are* happy and our prayer is this: "Thy will be my will, and may my will ever follow Thy will, and accord to it in all ways."

Nothing is farther from our thoughts than the dread words *submission, resignation.* To stay there would be dismal indeed,

> And, Lord, with a song,
>> Let my will
> Run all the day long
>> With Thy will.

That is life as we wish to live it.

But I do not find that this position, that of unbroken peacefulness and inward song, is one we can hope to hold unassailed. It is no soft arrangement of pillows, no easy chair. It is a fort in an enemy's country, and the foe is wise in assault and especially in surprise. And yet there can be nothing to fear, for it is not a place that we must keep, but a stronghold in which we are kept, if only, in the moment we are conscious of attack, we look "away unto our faith's princely leader and perfecter, Jesus, who endured" (Rotherham's rendering of Hebrews 12:2).

He who endured can protect and maintain that of which He is author and finisher: "Peace I leave with you, My peace I give unto you: not as the world giveth, give I unto you. Let not your heart be troubled, neither let it be afraid" (John 14:27).

This peace, no lesser, no other, is proof against the sharp stab of longing to be well again. The peace of God can keep us steady in the place where we most desire to dwell, so that we shall not shadow the lives of those who love us.

> If, in the paths of the world,
>> Stones might have wounded thy feet,
> Toil or dejection have tried
>> Thy Spirit, of that we saw nothing.

Of that we saw nothing—how good if, by His blessed enabling, we should daily so receive His peace that others should see nothing of stone, thorn, toil, dejection, but find, when they come, only the gift of great contentment, the restful peace of God. —*Rose From Brier*

QUESTIONS TO CONSIDER

1. What troubles your heart today? How is the way you're handling difficulty affecting those around you?

2. How can you experience more of God's peace?

A PRAYERFUL RESPONSE

Lord, please fill my heart with the desire and delight to do Your will. Amen.

A SOUL CAN SING

THOUGHT FOR TODAY

Your body may be bound, but your soul can sing.

WISDOM FROM SCRIPTURE

Praise be to the LORD my Rock, who trains my hands for war, my fingers for battle.

He is my loving God and my fortress, my stronghold and my deliverer, my shield, in whom I take refuge, who subdues peoples under me.

O LORD, what is man that you care for him, the son of man that you think of him? Man is like a breath; his days are like a fleeting shadow.

Part your heavens, O LORD, and come down; touch the mountains, so that they smoke. Send forth lightning and scatter the enemies; shoot your arrows and rout them.

Reach down your hand from on high; deliver me and rescue me from the mighty waters, from the hands of foreigners whose mouths are full of lies, whose right hands are deceitful.

I will sing a new song to you, O God; on the ten-stringed lyre I will make music to you, to the One who gives victory to kings, who delivers his servant David from the deadly sword.

Deliver me and rescue me from the hands of foreigners whose mouths are full of lies, whose right hands are deceitful. Then our sons in their youth will be like well-nurtured plants, and our daughters will be like pillars carved to adorn a palace.

Our barns will be filled with every kind of provision. Our sheep will increase by thousands, by tens of thousands in our fields; our oxen will draw heavy loads. There will be no breaching of walls, no going into captivity, no cry of distress in our streets.

Blessed are the people of whom this is true; blessed are the people whose God is the LORD.   PSALM 144, NIV

INSIGHTS FROM AMY CARMICHAEL

We have a little bird who has the pleasant custom of turning disturbing things into a cause for singing. The wind blows his bough and wakens him at midnight. His whole world is moving restlessly; he sings a tiny note or two then, perhaps to comfort himself. It is good to learn to do that.

Sometimes a song has come like coolness at the close of a hot day. The usual prayer meeting of the fellowship was going on in a room near mine. I could hear the singing; it was always comforting, but I could hear only the murmur of voices between prayer-songs and choruses. I did greatly long to be with my family there, and the filmy cloud of wish threatened to spread over my sky.

It had been such a sudden swing out of the life that had been very life to me for so many years, and I had not got accustomed to the change (nor have I yet, eleven months after that first sudden closing down of all joyous activities). I was turning over the pages of an old book, not with much brightness of spirit, but as a distraction from desire, when I came upon this: "On Himself shall His crown flourish" ("blossom" is Delitzch's word), "ever inflorescent, as a flower."

A blossoming crown—it was a delicately lovely little thought that floated into my room just then. It was like a flower or the petal of a flower blowing in on a light wind. They made His crown of thorns on that woeful day on Calvary, but He will be crowned with flowers one day. Perhaps some of them must be gathered on the fiery fields of pain.

But there were days when the throb of fleshly battle wound was lost in the sense of the throb of drums, as though heard from a long way off. Sometimes this victorious sound seemed to fill the air, and I all but saw the kingdoms of this world become the kingdoms of Christ our Lord. And songs came then about trumpets and bugles sounding afar, and about the triumph of our glorious King. Is it not a thought of exultation, that however crushed and crippled we may be, our leader is marching to music all the time, marching to a victory sure as the eternal heavens?

We follow a conqueror. We prisoners of the Lord follow hard after Him as He goes forth to His coronation. It is only our bodies that are bound. Our souls are free.

So the songs came. For by reasons of the "interior sweetness," as Richard Rolle says, "I was impelled to sing what before I had only said" to Him who hears the least little song of love. Such a song need not look for words, though sometimes the search for the right word can be strangely refreshing. Songs without words are songs to Him.   —*Rose From Brier*

QUESTIONS TO CONSIDER
1. What has caused you to feel crushed or crippled?
2. How can your soul be set free to sing?

A PRAYERFUL RESPONSE
Lord, set my soul free to sing love songs to You. Amen.

THE SPIRIT OF HAPPINESS

THOUGHT FOR TODAY

Thinking on "good things" develops the spirit of happiness.

WISDOM FROM SCRIPTURE

I will exalt you, my God the King; I will praise your name for ever and ever. Every day I will praise you and extol your name for ever and ever.

Great is the LORD and most worthy of praise; his greatness no one can fathom.

One generation will commend your works to another; they will tell of your mighty acts. They will speak of the glorious splendor of your majesty, and I will meditate on your wonderful works. They will tell of the power of your awesome works, and I will proclaim your great deeds. They will celebrate your abundant goodness and joyfully sing of your righteousness.

The LORD is gracious and compassionate, slow to anger and rich in love. The LORD is good to all; he has compassion on all he has made.

All you have made will praise you, O LORD; your saints will extol you. They will tell of the glory of your kingdom and speak of your might, so that all men may know of your mighty acts and the glorious splendor of your kingdom. Your kingdom is an everlasting kingdom, and your dominion endures through all generations.

The LORD is faithful to all his promises and loving toward all he has made. The LORD upholds all those who fall and lifts up all who are bowed down.

The eyes of all look to you, and you give them their food at the proper time. You open your hand and satisfy the desires of every living thing. The LORD is righteous in all his ways and loving toward all he has made.

The LORD is near to all who call on him, to all who call on him in truth. He fulfills the desires of those who fear him; he hears their cry and saves them.

The LORD watches over all who love him, but all the wicked he will destroy. My mouth will speak in praise of the LORD. Let every creature praise his holy name for ever and ever. PSALM 145, NIV

INSIGHTS FROM AMY CARMICHAEL

Can we ever thank God enough for the spirit of happiness? The spirit of happiness cannot be feigned. That spirit is genuine, or it is not there at all.

There is something in the continuance of happiness in untoward circumstances that is like the power of rejuvenescence in the rotifer. This little creature, which we find sometimes in a drop of water, is a thing so delicate that a slip of the cover-glass on the slide will destroy the pinpoint of life in its crystal vase. And yet, when the pond dries up, it can gather itself into a ball within which are the forces of life. Then after being blown about by the wind perhaps for years, in a state of utter dustiness, when the rotifer finds itself in its own element the ball will revive, and put forth foot and head and silver wheel, and be as it was before, a minute marvel of activity and apparent enjoyment.

The spirit of happiness is sheer miracle. It is the gift of the happy God, as Paul names our heavenly Father in writing to Timothy. It is the gift of the God of love. He pours it out of His own fountains, through unseen channels, as He poured it upon Paul and Silas before their feet were taken out of the stocks and their stripes washed; for "no created power in hell, or out of hell, can mar the music of our Lord Jesus, nor spoil our song of joy."

One of the great secrets of happiness is to think of happy things. There were many unhappy things in Philippi, things false, dishonorable, unjust, impure, hideous and of very bad report; the air of Philippi was darkened by these things. The Christians of that town might easily have had their lives stained by continually letting their thoughts dwell on what they could not help seeing and hearing and feeling, that evil they must often have met and fought in their striving together for the faith of the gospel.

But they were definitely told to think of things true, honorable, just, pure, lovely and of good report. "And if there be any virtue, and if there be any praise, think on these things" (Philippians 4:8). —*Gold by Moonlight*

Questions to Consider

1. Have you ever had your life "stained" by dwelling on negative or evil things? In what ways?

2. What could you think about that is true, honorable, just, pure, lovely or of good report?

A Prayerful Response

Lord, I will think on good things. Amen.

DAY 36

LET US CHERISH THANKFULNESS

THOUGHT FOR TODAY

You can be thankful, despite difficult circumstances.

WISDOM FROM SCRIPTURE

O give thanks to the LORD, for he is good, for his steadfast love endures forever.

O give thanks to the God of gods, for his steadfast love endures forever.

O give thanks to the Lord of lords, for his steadfast love endures forever; who alone does great wonders, for his steadfast love endures forever;

who by understanding made the heavens, for his steadfast love endures forever; who spread out the earth on the waters, for his steadfast love endures forever;

who made the great lights, for his steadfast love endures forever; the sun to rule over the day, for his steadfast love endures forever;

the moon and stars to rule over the night, for his steadfast love endures forever;

who struck Egypt through their firstborn, for his steadfast love endures forever;

and brought Israel out from among them, for his steadfast love endures forever;

with a strong hand and an outstretched arm, for his steadfast love endures forever;

who divided the Red Sea in two, for his steadfast love endures forever;

and made Israel pass through the midst of it, for his steadfast love endures forever;

but overthrew Pharaoh and his army in the Red Sea, for his steadfast love endures forever;

who led his people through the wilderness, for his steadfast love endures forever;

who struck down great kings, for his steadfast love endures forever;

It is he who remembered us in our low estate, for his steadfast love endures forever;

and rescued us from our foes, for his steadfast love endures forever;

who gives food to all flesh, for his steadfast love endures forever.

O give thanks to the God of heaven, for his steadfast love endures forever.   PSALMS 136:1-17, 23-26, RSV

INSIGHTS FROM AMY CARMICHAEL

"In everything give thanks."   1 THESSALONIANS 5:18

This is a constant word to me. It is so easy to give thanks for what one naturally chooses, but that does not cover the "every thing" of the text.

I have read of John Bunyan making a flute from the leg of his stool. When his jailer came to stop him playing on this queer flute, he slipped it back in its place in his stool.

The joy of the Lord is an unquenchable thing. It does not depend upon circumstances, or upon place, or upon health (though health is a tremendous help to joy), or upon our being able to do what we want to do. It is like our river. It has its source high up among the mountains, and the little happenings down in the riverbed do not affect it.

One morning lately, in speaking of some small trouble, I quoted, "In everything give thanks," and at once someone answered, "But I cannot give thanks for everything." Now, if our God tells us to do a thing and we say cannot there is something wrong somewhere, for we all know the words, "I can do all things through Christ which strengtheneth me" (Philippians 4:13)—that is, all things commanded. It is treason to say, "I cannot." But first we should make sure that we are commanded to do this that we feel we cannot do.

I do not think we are to give thanks *for* everything. To make sure of this verse which is sometimes quoted with "for" instead of "in," I looked it up in seven versions. In six of the seven it is *in;* only one version has *for.* So I take it that we may understand the word to mean, not "Give thanks *for* everything," but "Give thanks *in* everything," which is a different matter.

All God's biddings are enablings. We can do that. *We will do that.*

Let us cherish thankfulness.   HEBREWS 12:28, WEYMOUTH

I think thankfulness is like a flower. It needs care and cherishing if it is to live and grow. Perhaps thankfulness, even more than some other qualities that seem to come naturally to us, is in need of cherishing, because of the withering winds of life.

The best way to cause it to grow in our hearts is to be careful never to let ourselves be *un*thankful. Has anyone done anything to help me and I have said nothing about it? (It is not enough to thank God; we should thank the one to whom He gave the loving thought that caused the loving deed.) Has anyone prepared a surprise for me and I have been blind to it? Or if I noticed it, have I been dumb? If we have been careless about this, let us put it right.

I often think we must disappoint our kind Father by not noticing the little things (as well as the countless great things) that He does to give us pleasure. Perhaps we should begin by thinking more of what His children do for love of Him and for love of us too.

As I read in Hebrews I came upon a cause for very great thankfulness that I had not noticed before. Suppose the Old Testament promises were only for those to whom they were first given; suppose we had no right to take them to ourselves (some say this is so); what a tremendous loss it would be.

Hebrews 13:5 was the word that brought this home to me just now. There we have the essence of three glorious Old Testament verses of truth and comfort belonging to other people, given to us for our own use. I take it that the Spirit of God guided the writer of Hebrews, both in the choice of his quotations and in the translation of them, so that we have the very words that can help us most: "I will in no wise fail thee, neither will I in any wise forsake thee" from Genesis 28:15, Deuteronomy 31:6, 8 and Joshua 1:5. Then, "The Lord is my helper; I will not fear: what shall man do unto me?" from Psalms 118:6 and Psalms 56:9-13.

What can man, or devil, or my own self do to me, if I may truly know that the Lord of heaven and earth is my Helper, and that He truly says to me, "I will in no wise fail thee, neither will I in any wise forsake thee"?

So let us cherish thankfulness. "In God's word will I rejoice; in the Lord's word will I comfort me" (Psalms 56:10). "For though my soul is among lions every day of its life, with me is the most high God that shall perform the cause which I have in mind" (Psalms 57:2, 4).   —*Thou Givest... They Gather*

QUESTIONS TO CONSIDER

1. Why do we need to cherish thankfulness? How can we do it?

2. How can Amy's insight that "All God's biddings are enablings" help you in a difficult circumstance?

A PRAYERFUL RESPONSE

Lord, I will give thanks to You amidst today's circumstances. Amen.

MELODY IN OUR HEAVINESS

THOUGHT FOR TODAY

God hears your prayers as songs to Him.

WISDOM FROM SCRIPTURE

Praise the LORD. Praise the name of the LORD; praise him, you servants of the LORD, you who minister in the house of the LORD, in the courts of the house of our God.

Praise the LORD, for the LORD is good; sing praise to his name, for that is pleasant. For the LORD has chosen Jacob to be his own, Israel to be his treasured possession.

I know that the LORD is great, that our LORD is greater than all gods.

The LORD does whatever pleases him, in the heavens and on the earth, in the seas and all their depths.

He makes clouds rise from the ends of the earth; he sends lightning with the rain and brings out the wind from his storehouses. He struck down the firstborn of Egypt, the firstborn of men and animals.

He sent his signs and wonders into your midst, O Egypt, against Pharaoh and all his servants. He struck down many nations and killed mighty kings—Sihon king of the Amorites, Og king of Bashan and all the kings of Canaan—and he gave their land as an inheritance, an inheritance to his people Israel.

Your name, O LORD, endures forever, your renown, O LORD, through all generations.

For the LORD will vindicate his people and have compassion on his servants.

The idols of the nations are silver and gold, made by the hands of men. They have mouths, but cannot speak, eyes, but they cannot see; they have ears, but cannot hear, nor is there breath in their mouths. Those who make them will be like them, and so will all who trust in them.

O house of Israel, praise the LORD; O house of Aaron, praise the LORD; O house of Levi, praise the LORD; you who fear him, praise the LORD.

Praise be to the LORD from Zion, to him who dwells in Jerusalem. Praise the LORD.   PSALM 135, NIV

INSIGHTS FROM AMY CARMICHAEL

Melody in our heaviness.   PSALMS 137:3

I do not think that such heaviness as was felt by the people who were led captive into Babylon is meant to be lightened by melody; but there is another kind of heaviness: the tired-out feeling that may come, and that our Lord knew when He sat on the well (John 4:6).

I am quite sure that sometimes this kind of heaviness has to be. If it were not so, we should not know how to help other tired people. These words, "melody in our heaviness," show us one of the quickest ways out of the heaviness that depresses the spirit, even though all may be clear between us and our Lord.

Try melody—try singing. If you cannot sing aloud, sing in your heart, "singing and making melody in your heart to the Lord" (Ephesians 5:19).

Sometimes we cannot sing much, but we can look up to our God and say a word or two. I did not know till one day last week that He calls that little word a song. In the Revised Version of Psalms 42:8 we have this: "In the night His song shall be with me, even a prayer unto the God of my life." (Other versions have the same thought: *Prayer is song to God.*)

"If thou be tempted, rise thou on the wings of prayer to thy beloved," and He will take that poor little prayer and turn it into a song.

From the midst of frustrations in Central Africa, Fred Arnot, who was the Livingstone of those regions, wrote, "I am learning never to be disappointed, but to praise."

I read that journal letter of his when it came home—it must be more than forty years ago—but that vital word in an ordinary letter remained with me, ready for a moment of need. *I am learning never to be disappointed, but to praise.*

God keeps us so near to Himself that there will be little shining seeds like that scattered about our letters—seeds that will bear a harvest of joy somewhere, sometime, and be melody to others in their heaviness.

> *He parted from them and they returned to Jerusalem with great joy.* Luke 24:51-52

I have often said that there is nothing in Scripture to encourage us to live the life that has what it desires, and frets if it cannot have it. There is no provision made for a life of that kind. Always we are expected to live triumphantly without what we would naturally wish for most; and full provision is made for that kind of life.

The words quoted above show this perfectly. He whom they most desired, He whose preciousness they understood as they never had before, was parted from them, "and they worshiped Him, and returned to Jerusalem [where any day they might

156

have to suffer for His sake] with great joy: and were continually in the temple [not weakened by longings for what they could not have, but] praising and blessing God."

—*Thou Givest... They Gather*

QUESTIONS TO CONSIDER

1. What do you want that you don't have? How does this make you feel?

2. How can you turn your heaviness into a song?

A PRAYERFUL RESPONSE

Lord, I will praise You, even though I don't have everything I want in life. Amen.

PART SIX

THE WORLD TO COME

Will not the End explain
The crossed endeavor, earnest purpose foiled,
The strong bewilderment of good work spoiled,
The clinging weariness, the inner strain,
Will not the End explain?

Meanwhile He comforteth
Them that are losing patience; 'tis His way.
But none can write the words they hear Him say,
For men to read; only they know He saith
Kind words, and comforteth.

Not that He doth explain
The mystery that baffleth; but a sense
Husheth the quiet heart, that far, far hence
Lieth a field set thick with golden grain,
Wetted in seedling days by many a rain;
The End, it will explain.

"THE END," *TOWARD JERUSALEM*

AMY CARMICHAEL'S INSIGHT

You may not understand all of earth's pain until you reach
the blessings of heaven and the delight of His countenance.

MORNING GLORY

THOUGHT FOR TODAY

Don't lose the hope of God's glory to come.

WISDOM FROM SCRIPTURE

Praise awaits you, O God, in Zion; to you our vows will be fulfilled.

O you who hear prayer, to you all men will come. When we were overwhelmed by sins, you forgave our transgressions.

Blessed are those you choose and bring near to live in your courts! We are filled with the good things of your house, of your holy temple.

You answer us with awesome deeds of righteousness, O God our Savior, the hope of all the ends of the earth and of the farthest seas, who formed the mountains by your power, having armed yourself with strength, who stilled the roaring of the seas, the roaring of their waves, and the turmoil of the nations.

Those living far away fear your wonders; where morning dawns and evening fades you call forth songs of joy.

You care for the land and water it; you enrich it abundantly. The streams of God are filled with water to provide the people with grain, for so you have ordained it. You drench its furrows and level its ridges; you soften it with showers and bless its crops.

You crown the year with your bounty, and your carts overflow with abundance.

The grasslands of the desert overflow; the hills are clothed with gladness. The meadows are covered with flocks and the valleys are mantled with grain; they shout for joy and sing.   PSALM 65, NIV

INSIGHTS FROM AMY CARMICHAEL

And now, Lord, what do I wait for? My hope is in Thee. The shadows of evening are stretched out. The clouds are heavy on the mountains. Thou touchest the hills and they smoke.

But like all the clouds of all my life, these heavy clouds are edged with light; and when I look up to the highest cloud I see there no darkness at all, but light, and light beyond light shining down on the peaceful water.

And the water—for I have said to Thee, "Bid me come unto Thee on the water," and Thou hast said, "Come"—that water is a pathway of light.

I see a narrow break in the brightness because of the cloud overhead, but soon it is bright again, and then there is no more shadow. And far, far, all but lost in light, I see what I think are other hills, the hills of a better country, even a heavenly one.

One evening, as we sat at the end of India on the rocks of Cape Comorin, a little fishing boat sailed into the sunset. It was only a rough thing made of three logs tied together, and its sail was a mere rag, but it was transfigured. To see it was like seeing the mortal put on immortality, the temporal take on the beauty of the eternal.

Usually, I think, a speck of earth entangled in such glory would dare show against the glory, but that evening, so mighty was the power of the golden air, that all of earth was swallowed up. It held us speechless. As I think of it I hear again the lapping of the waves that filled the solace and see the lighted waters in the afterglow.

But what we call sunset the heavenly people call sunrise, and the joy of the Lord, and the morning of God.

—*Gold by Moonlight*

QUESTIONS TO CONSIDER

1. How can you anticipate God's glory to come?
2. How can you experience His glory in everyday life?

A PRAYERFUL RESPONSE

Lord, I will fix my eyes on the glory to come in heaven. Amen.

FOR WE SHALL SEE HIM

THOUGHT FOR TODAY

In heaven there will be no more pain and trouble.

WISDOM FROM SCRIPTURE

"See, I am coming soon! Blessed is the one who keeps the words of the prophecy of this book."

I, John, am the one who heard and saw these things. And when I heard and saw them, I fell down to worship at the feet of the angel who showed them to me; but he said to me, "You must not do that! I am a fellow servant with you and your comrades the prophets, and with those who keep the words of this book. Worship God!"

And he said to me, "Do not seal up the words of the prophecy of this book, for the time is near.

"Let the evildoer still do evil, and the filthy still be filthy, and the righteous still do right, and the holy still be holy."

"See, I am coming soon; my reward is with me, to repay according to everyone's work.

"I am the Alpha and the Omega, the first and the last, the beginning and the end."

Blessed are those who wash their robes, so that they will have the right to the tree of life and may enter the city by the gates.

Outside are the dogs and sorcerers and fornicators and murderers and idolaters, and everyone who loves and practices falsehood.

"It is I, Jesus, who sent my angel to you with this testimony for the churches. I am the root and the descendant of David, the bright morning star."

The Spirit and the bride say, "Come." And let everyone who hears say, "Come." And let everyone who is thirsty come. Let anyone who wishes take the water of life as a gift.

REVELATION 22:7-17, RSV

INSIGHTS FROM AMY CARMICHAEL

Every child asks, "What will heaven be like?" Every grown-up child seeks among the glories and beauties of the earth—sunrise skies, sunsets, all sinless loveliness, music that carries the soul to His feet—for something approaching an answer, till it at last settles down on *"Eye hath not seen, nor ear heard"* (1 Corinthians 2:9).

But certain words grow to mean heaven to us. These are my heaven-words: "We shall be like Him, for we shall see Him as He is" (1 John 3:2). "And His servants shall serve Him: and they shall see His face; and His name shall be in their foreheads" (Revelation 22:3-4).

All other luminous words scattered through prophets, psalms, the gospels, the epistles and Revelation, gather round these words and shine on them till they become as "pure gold, like unto clear glass," and we, looking through, see into heaven.

And till then? I do not understand the Book of Revelation as I wish I did, but chapter 12 shows the triumph of righteousness: "Therefore rejoice, ye heavens" (12:12). Chapter 13 shows the triumph of unrighteousness, and the word that sums things up is this: "Here is the patience and the faith of the saints" (13:10). "Here is an opportunity for endurance, and for the exercise of faith, on the part of God's people" (Weymouth).

Our Lord has conquered sin and pain and death. "Rejoice, ye heavens," and let us rejoice, too, for nothing can shake that glorious fact. And the day is racing toward us when we shall see Him and be like Him.

Till that day comes, "Here is an opportunity for endurance, and for the exercise of faith." May the Lord strengthen us all to buy up that opportunity—every minute of it.

—Thou Givest... They Gather

QUESTIONS TO CONSIDER

1. How can you exercise your faith as you wait for heaven?

2. How do you envision eternal life without pain or trouble?

A PRAYERFUL RESPONSE

Lord, thank You that someday I will be with You and troubles will cease. Amen.

TRUST AND FEAR NOT

THOUGHT FOR TODAY

You can trust God with your life.

WISDOM FROM SCRIPTURE

He who dwells in the shelter of the Most High will rest in the shadow of the Almighty.

I will say of the LORD, "He is my refuge and my fortress, my God, in whom I trust."

Surely he will save you from the fowler's snare and from the deadly pestilence. He will cover you with his feathers, and under his wings you will find refuge; his faithfulness will be your shield and rampart.

You will not fear the terror of night, nor the arrow that flies by day, nor the pestilence that stalks in the darkness, nor the plague that destroys at midday.

A thousand may fall at your side, ten thousand at your right hand, but it will not come near you. You will only observe with your eyes and see the punishment of the wicked.

If you make the Most High your dwelling—even the LORD, who is my refuge—then no harm will befall you, no disaster will come near your tent.

For he will command his angels concerning you to guard you in all your ways; they will lift you up in their hands, so that you will not strike your foot against a stone. You will tread upon the lion and the cobra; you will trample the great lion and the serpent.

"Because he loves me," says the LORD, "I will rescue him;

I will protect him, for he acknowledges my name. He will call upon me, and I will answer him; I will be with him in trouble, I will deliver him and honor him. With long life will I satisfy him and show him my salvation."

Psalm 91, NIV

Insights from Amy Carmichael

Let us end on a very simple note. Let us listen to simple words; our Lord speaks simply: "Trust Me, My child." He says, "Trust Me with a humbler heart and a fuller abandon to My will than ever thou didst before.

"Trust Me to pour My love through thee, as minute succeeds minute. And if thou shouldst be conscious of anything hindering the flow, do not hurt My love by going away from Me in discouragement, for nothing can hurt love so much as that.

"Draw all the closer to Me; come, flee unto Me to hide thee, even from thyself. Tell Me about the trouble. Trust Me to turn My hand upon thee and thoroughly remove the boulder that has choked thy riverbed, and take away all the sand that has silted up the channel.

"I will not leave thee until I have done what I have spoken to thee of. I will perfect what concerneth thee. Fear thou not, O child of My love; fear not."

Lord, what is love?

Love is what inspired My life, and led Me to My cross, and held Me on My cross. Love is what will make it thy joy to lay down thy life for thy brethren.

Lord, evermore give me this love.

Blessed are they who hunger and thirst after love, for they shall be filled.

Amen, Lord Jesus.   —*If*

QUESTIONS TO CONSIDER

1. Do you sense God's love pouring through you? If not, what might be hindering its flow?

2. What can you do to increase the flow of God's love into your life?

A PRAYERFUL RESPONSE

Lord, I trust You with my life and future. Amen.

REFERENCE NOTES

Throughout her books Amy Carmichael referred to various spiritual sources contemporary to her times. Unfortunately, Amy didn't cite full references, so it's difficult to know exactly what sources she casually refers to in her teachings.

To help today's reader, this list is a "best guess" of the sources Amy may have been reading and quoting in her books. The compiler apologizes for any inaccuracies.

Authorized Version: The King James Version of the *Holy Bible,* published in 1611.

Buchan, John: Author (1875–1940) of the book *Oliver Cromwell,* published in 1934. Cromwell (1599–1658) was an English soldier and statesman, named "Lord Protector of the Commonwealth" in 1653.

Bunyan, John: Author (1628–1688) of the classic *Pilgrim's Progress,* written during his twelve-year imprisonment for refusing to conform to the Church of England.

Darby: John Nelson Darby (1800–1882), lecturer and author of expositions on books of the Bible.

Delitzsch: The German Franz Delitzsch (1813–1890), author of commentaries on Old Testament books and a translation of the New Testament from the Hebrew.

Guyon, Madame: Jeanne Marie Bouvier de La Motte Guyon (1648–1717), a French noblewoman imprisoned for her faith in God.

Hannington: James Hannington (1847–1885), an English missionary and bishop in East Africa, martyred by Ugandan soldiers.

Julian of Norwich: Dame Julian of Norwich (ca. 1342–ca. 1416), a reclusive mystical writer from England.

Kay: Unable to determine this source.

Menicus: A Chinese philosopher (ca. 372 B.C.–ca. 289 B.C.) who followed Confucius and earned the title "Second Sage," as second only to Confucius in wisdom.

Moffatt: An English Bible published by James Moffat in 1926.

Moule: Horace Frederick Moule, coauthor of a historical catalog of printed editions of the Bible, published in 1903.

Prayer Book Version: From the Psalter included with *The Book of Common Prayer* published by the Church of England or the Protestant Episcopal Church.

Revelation of Divine Love: Book about the sinful chasms between humanity and Christ, written by Dame Julian of Norwich.

Revised Version: The Revised Version of the *Holy Bible*, published in 1884.

Rolle, Richard: Mystic and writer (ca. 1290–1349) from England.

Rotherham: Joseph Bryant Rotherham (1828–1910), translator and author of *The Emphasized Bible,* "a translation designed to set forth the exact meaning, the proper terminology and the graphic style of the sacred original."

Rutherford, Samuel: A Scottish preacher (1600–1661) exiled for his defense of Calvinism, the "doctrines of grace."

Weymouth: Richard Francis Weymouth (1822–1902), translator and author of *The New Testament in Modern Speech,* an idiomatic translation into everyday English from the Greek.

Young: Robert Young (1822–1888), translator and author of an analytical concordance to the Bible, designed for the readers of his English Bible.

BOOKS BY AMY CARMICHAEL

Candles in the Dark
Edges of His Ways
Figures of the True
God's Missionary
Gold by Moonlight
Gold Cord
His Thoughts Said… His Father Said…
If
Learning of God
Mimosa
Rose From Brier
Thou Givest . . . They Gather
Toward Jerusalem
Whispers of His Power

BOOKS ABOUT AMY CARMICHAEL

A Chance to Die
Amy Carmichael of Dohnavur

ABOUT THE COMPILER

With the *Life Messages of Great Christians* devotional series, Judith Couchman hopes you'll be encouraged and enlightened by people who've shared their spiritual journeys through the printed word.

Judith owns Judith & Company, a writing and editorial consulting business. She has also served as the creator and founding editor-in-chief of *Clarity* magazine, managing editor of *Christian Life*, editor of *Sunday Digest*, director of communications for The Navigators, and director of new product development for NavPress.

Besides speaking to women's and professional conferences, Judith has published ten books and many magazine articles. In addition, she has received numerous awards for her work in secondary education, religious publishing, and corporate communications.

She lives in Colorado.